ANYBODY WHO OWNS
HIS OWN HOME
DESERVES IT

ANYBODY WHO OWNS
HIS OWN HOME
DESERVES IT

by
ALAN KING

with
KATHRYN RYAN

E. P. DUTTON & CO., Inc.
New York   1962

CONTENTS

FOREWORD

ALL I EVER WANTED was a nice comfortable apartment in the city, with somebody else to take out the garbage, and somebody else to worry about the heat. Instead, for the past eleven years, I've been a member—against my will—of the suburban community.

The experience has not been without some value. For instance, where else would I have earned the right to be called The Crabgrass Comic, or the General de Gaulle of the commuter set? What other spokesman of the suburban scene argues more loudly about it? Who suffers more than I?

This book is an effort to show how I got trapped in Suburbia and to give you my impressions of life in the Station Wagon Age. If it frightens some of you back to the city, you have my envious best wishes. If, after reading this book, the rest of you commuters decide to stay on in your mortgaged mansions, don't say I didn't warn you. And don't come looking to me for sympathy, I've got troubles enough of my own.

As far as I'm concerned, anybody who owns his own home—deserves it.

ANYBODY WHO OWNS
HIS OWN HOME
DESERVES IT

[1] Daddy,
Buy Me a House

ON WINTER NIGHTS when city people are enjoying themselves at a cocktail party or a play, I sit snowbound at
home and meditate about all the strategies my wife
used to trap me into buying a house in the country.
What am I doing here? I ask myself. A man who is
contented in the city, who loved his apartment, who
was only a fifty-cent cab ride from Lindy's. How did
I *ever* let Jeanette talk me into this?

We both grew up in the city—and I thought we both loved city life. We had a handsome new apartment overlooking Central Park where the Sanitation Department took care of the garbage and the landlord worried about the heat. It was an idyllic existence— or so *I* thought.

We'd been in the new apartment only six months when she began dropping the first hints. One day she said to me, "I don't know what it is, but I just feel stifled. I feel so confined in these surroundings."

I suggested she take off her girdle and spread out a little. She gave me a nasty look and stalked out of the room.

She suddenly started complaining about everything. "Close the window," she told me one afternoon. It was July 8th and maybe 100 degrees outside.

"You want me to close the window?" I asked incredulously.

"The dirt and the soot just keep coming in. No matter how often I clean, the rooms still look grimy," she told me, "and besides, the street noises are driving me crazy."

A few days later she came up with a new one: "I have such an overwhelming desire to get my hands on some good earth." That one was easy. I went out and bought her the book. I *do* come up with some answers.

She tossed it aside and looked sorrowfully at me.

"I'm talking about garden loam," she said. "Alan, aren't you interested in roses and violets and daisies?"

"What for? I'm not in the millinery business."

When the agent came to collect the rent—as was his habit—she said, "Alan, why pay rent? We could be saving this money." I ignored her.

Finally she used the direct approach and the most persuasive one, the one she always uses to get her own way—crying.

"I want a house," she wailed. "We can't live here any more."

I exploded. "What's wrong with this?" I asked her. "Is this a tent?"

"Oh, Alan," she was still in tears, "I just don't have any friends here any more. Everybody's moving to the suburbs."

She made it sound like an exodus. I guess somebody cut a ribbon, fired a pistol, and the land rush was on. I could just see those gallant pioneers on Queens Boulevard in their covered wagons with the mink stoles hanging out the back, yelling, "Onward to the Suburbs!"

"I am not buying a house," I told her.

Then there came the afternoon when she got carried away. "Think of the children," she yelled at me. This confused me a little because we didn't have any kids at the time. My big mistake was in pointing this out to her.

A few weeks later she woke me up in the middle of the night. Now most men know that when a woman has anything important to tell you, she doesn't get around to it during the dinner hour or in the early evening. She waits 'til you're sound asleep. *Then* she remembers she has something to tell you.

I suppose one of the reasons for this is that most women don't sleep too well at night. In the morning and afternoon they lie there like they're dead, but at night they don't sleep. My wife watches the Late Show and the Late, Late Show, then she salutes the flag and sings "The Star-Spangled Banner." She never leaves 'til the dot disappears. She can even watch two hours of snow. Then, with nothing else to do, she starts giving me her attention. If it were up to me, I'd have television twenty-four hours a day.

On this particular night she walked into the bedroom and saw me lying there. But she apparently decided that I wasn't sleeping. I was playing possum. It was four o'clock in the morning, so what would I be kidding about? I'm rather peculiar—I'm either sleeping or I'm not. But Jeanette doesn't like to take any chances. That night, as always, she had to put me through the test.

She turned on all the lights, slammed the door a couple of times, ran the shower, and gave a polite cough as though she were losing a lung. Then she asked, "Alan, are you awake?"

"If I was in a coma, I'd react a little bit," I told her.

She jumped on the bed and dug an elbow into my ribs. "Alan, if you're not doing anything—"

14

Well, you know, four in the morning— "I'm always busy at this hour, Jeanette," I told her. "I play polo every morning at four o'clock. Now what do you want?"

"I don't know what it is," she said, "but I'm so hungry. I just feel like having some exotic food. Get up and run down to the all-night delicatessen."

"*Run* down to the all-night delicatessen? Are you crazy?"

"I just feel like exotic food," she insisted.

"Why don't you have some Corn Flakes? I'll sing a Hawaiian war chant for you."

"No," she said, "I just have an urge. I'd like a corned-beef sandwich with whipped cream and chocolate sprinkles, and a piece of watermelon and a sour pickle."

Well, you realize that, sleepy as I was, I knew that this was it, because even if she wasn't pregnant, this could start it. I had never heard of a menu like this.

She began to cry. "We can't bring up our children here," she sobbed. "We've got to move to the country."

"Look," I tried to reason with her, "it's four in the morning. We're not moving anywhere."

"I will not have my children—"

"What *my* children? You don't even know if you're pregnant. Maybe it's gas. We'll save a little money."

"This is no place to raise kids," she told me.

"Jeanette, I've had about enough of this. Let the kid come. If he doesn't like it, let *him* buy a house in the country. I'm staying right here."

Fourteen months later our son Bobby was born. My

wife had the longest pregnancy on record. My guess is that she wasn't pregnant the night she made up that menu. For a while I think she waited around to see if a baby was absolutely essential to her plan—and *then* she went ahead with it. She's very clever that way.

The baby was really something. He was a little roly-poly with the cutest smile you ever saw. He looked like me—and we hit it off from the start. When I'd come in he'd reach up and grab my finger in his fat little hand and hold on for dear life.

I was beginning to enjoy fatherhood. I hate to brag, but he was the smartest six-months-old baby you ever saw. Do you know that one day I came home and Jeanette came running out to meet me. "Alan," she said, breathlessly, "the baby said his first words today."

"What'd he say?" I asked, excitedly.

"I distinctly heard him say, 'Daddy, buy me a house.'"

❋ ❋ ❋

"Mr. Fieldston will see you now," said the pretty blonde secretary.

We crossed the thickly carpeted room and knocked at the paneled door with the thin, elegant gold letters which read, "Harvey Fieldston."

"Oh, Alan, I'm so excited," Jeanette said. "Mr. Fieldston is the biggest real-estate agent on Long Island." And, as it turned out, she was right.

Harvey Fieldston drove us out to look at a place he had in mind. It was Sunday and there was bumper-to-bumper traffic.

"How far is this house from the city?" I asked, as we crawled along.

"Only a twenty-minute drive, Mr. King," said Fieldston.

That's if they shoot you out on an Atlas missile.

When we finally arrived, the house turned out to be a California contemporary nestled in a sleepy, pastoral little community of four hundred and fifty other houses that looked exactly like it. The development was called God's Little Acre, and I found out only He could afford it. The house was loosely described as a ranch-type, and it's designs like this that could start the Indian war all over again.

We bought the house for $33,000. It was listed to sell for $12,500 but we wanted extras. We needed windows, we wanted a floor, and I thought since we were going this far it would be a nice idea to have a roof over our heads. It was a real steal, according to Fieldston. The only question in my mind was who was stealing from whom?

Our new acquisition had seven rooms and two bathrooms so we were *really* moving up. Of course, I found out that I could use only one bathroom. The other was a guest bathroom. Even if we didn't have guests, I was never allowed to go into that one.

As soon as we got all the "extras," we moved right in since, according to my wife, the baby couldn't last much longer in the apartment. This meant I had to pay up another ten months of my lease to get out of the apartment, but Jeanette was very happy.

So quite suddenly I found myself a country squire— a land baron. My entire estate was 80 x 100 feet. My great-grandfather is buried in a bigger plot than we lived on. But this, my wife claimed, was gracious living. With two hours' commuting a day, hundreds of chores, and just enough sleep to survive on, I found out I had about forty minutes a day for gracious living.

Now as we quickly found out, you don't just move in, settle back, and enjoy your well-earned peace in the suburbs. Life in the suburbs is *not* a private affair. In our city apartment we could go for days without seeing anyone, if that was what we wanted. There is a pleasant anonymity to life in the city. You can walk down the streets and not really notice the crowds of people who aren't really noticing you. The rush and noise of a big city are impersonal things. They don't infringe unless you want them to. In the suburbs, it's different. You get invaded—by friend and foe alike.

The first scouts were the Welcome Wagon ladies. They arrived four hours after we did. Now these are usually a couple of clubwomen who have nothing better to do than annoy people. They hustle for the local merchants. They give you very valuable gifts like a car wash. Well, it isn't a car wash, exactly. What you get is the right to use the water in the gas station if you get there before six o'clock in the morning. We also got a dandelion duster, a coaster which says, "Drink Ballantine Beer," and a coupon that entitled us to a free nail file from the local drugstore after our first ten-dollar purchase.

Next came the spearhead of the invasion—an oil man, who arrived to fill the tank, and two specialists from the gas company. One adjusted only burner flames on kitchen stoves and the other worked only on pilot lights.

This trend toward specialization is becoming ridiculous. I called in an electrician to put up a light over the entrance to the garage. It seemed simple enough to me. "I'd like a light here," I told him.

"Well," he said, "we'll have to run in a BX cable."

"What BX? I just want a little light."

"You don't understand, sir," he told me. "This is an outside connection. You have to run it from the main line and cut through the lawn."

"No," I said, "it's just a small bulb I want."

"You don't seem to get it, buddy," he said. "You need a BX cable and you have to run it from the main line that comes in from the street. You have to dig a trench in the lawn."

All this for a forty-watt bulb? "Look," I told him,

19

"you want to just forget about it? I'll hang a flashlight from the roof."

Our entire first month in the house went pretty much like that. We were besieged by salesmen, shown up by specialists, and intimidated by the neighbors—the last in a frightening sort of way.

The first week we were in the house I discovered that the most important appearance of status in the suburbs is the lawn. There's an unofficial contest to see who has the nicest lawn. The women make up the rules, but the husbands are the contestants.

My introduction to the game came on the first Sunday after we'd moved in. I'd come home about five A.M. after working all night in a club, gone right to bed and to sleep. Sometime later I heard a sound like motorboats revving up outside. I jumped out of bed and ran to the window. It was seven in the morning and all up and down the block my neighbors were tuning up their power mowers, preparatory to cutting the grass.

Now these were apparently sane, sober men from Monday through Saturday. On Sunday they changed. Every one of them was wearing The Outfit—Bermuda shorts with high socks ending at bony knees, leather-thonged sandals, and a shirt with an alligator on the pocket. That's the sign, apparently, by which one affluent homeowner recognizes another. In this ridiculous attire my neighbors started to work on the lawns.

They were all bright and fresh—happy as larks with

their power mowers. You don't have to drink much in the suburbs, you know. You can get loaded on fertilizer. I leaned out the window, hoping to get at least one of them to stop. My next-door neighbor spotted me. "Whaddya gonna do about the crabgrass?" he bawled, pointing to my lawn.

No hello. No "welcome to the neighborhood." Just a slur on my lawn.

"Well," I told him, "I'll tell you the truth. I don't make big decisions at seven o'clock in the morning. I'm gonna let it lay there until three, and *then* I'll decide what to do with it."

"I hope your lawn rots," he yelled back.

"And I hope it spreads to everybody else's lawn," I informed him. "I'd like to wish the world a fungus infection."

🌺 🌺 🌺

I was still finding my way around the house when Jeanette said, "We've got to add on a room." Now we had more rooms than both our families put together and I thought she must be kidding. But I found out that the neighbors were doing it, and she had to keep up with them. They weren't adding rooms, exactly; they were enclosing porches. There was one house in the neighborhood that consisted of a bathroom, a kitchen, and eleven closed-in porches.

21

We enclosed a porch of our own and made that into a den. Then the room we were using for a den we made into another guest bedroom. Our second son, Andy, was born a little later so we gave each boy his own room. Jeanette was absolutely insistent on that. "The neighbors will talk," she said. So they had separate rooms, which meant that they always slept in the same room anyway.

My role in the house was important right from the start, just as it is today. My wife found me absolutely essential for two reasons: to earn the money she needed for all of her schemes, and to dispose of the garbage.

I honestly think she had the house wired before we moved in so she could locate me fast. The minute I sat down, she knew it.

"Alan," she'd call, "get up and take out the garbage."

I'd be understandably confused because we hadn't eaten. I always wondered where the hell the garbage was coming from. I really believe she collected the garbage from the neighbors just so I could take it out for her. As a matter of fact, she still does. Either that or she buys Instant Garbage. You add a little water and you've got all the garbage you need.

This is Gracious Living?

I've saved my money all my life just so I could become my own janitor.

[2] Thank You,
Act One

I'VE NEVER WORRIED MUCH about my career because I believe I have all the requisites for success. I'm the son of Russian emigrant parents, one of a large family of seven boys and a girl; I ran away from home at an early age; I peddled papers and sang on street corners for pennies; I was born and raised in the tenement section of the lower East Side of New York.

How could I miss?

I guess every comedian in America was born on the lower East Side of New York. That's why it was so crowded down there. I know a comedian from Canton, Ohio, who moved to the lower East Side at the age of thirty-six, just so he'd have something to talk about.

For example:

"We lived so far downtown, 14th Street was like Connecticut to us."

"We were so poor we lived **below** the candy store."

"My parents couldn't afford to have another child—so a neighbor had me."   And,

"In this neighborhood you either grew up to be a judge or you got the chair."

(End of monologue)

My wife, Jeanette, lived in the same neighborhood. Of course to look at my wife today, you'd never *dream* she came from such humble beginnings—unless you talked to her. At first glance she gives the impression of being transplanted from a plantation in Virginia.

I think one of the reasons she's not too happy with me is because I'm the only one left who remembers where she came from. I even have a picture of her old nose. Please believe me, I'm not being cruel; this is simply the only defense I have left. When she steps out of line, I flash our wedding picture. "Remember?"

Even though we were childhood sweethearts, Jeanette's parents were dead set against our marriage. Her father wanted her to marry a doctor. That's all I ever used to hear. To this day I don't know what grudge he had against the medical profession.

When we got married my family had more money than her family and we were on relief, so you can imagine what a successful group she belonged to.

I will not discuss my mother-in-law here because this book is in a humorous vein, and my mother-in-law just doesn't have one.

My wife has one brother, Murray, whom I just might mention a little later. The last real honest job he had was selling *Liberty* magazines. If I were forced to give a capsule description of Murray I would have to say that he's the kind of a fellow who gets a job as an usher at Ebbets Field *now*.

My wife also has a sister who is just a younger edition of the same thing I have to put up with every day. Being so much alike, they are very close. They visit each other every day and then they get on the phone for four or five hours to pass away the rest of the time. In fact they're on the phone so continuously that if I call home and the phone rings, I get panicky! I know something's wrong. I can always tell when Jeanette's talking to her sister because when I walk into the room, she always says, "I can't talk to you now. *He's* here!"

My family was also very close, not by choice, but from necessity. We lived in a four-room flat and I slept in the same bed with four brothers and some guy we didn't even know.

I was raised with the love and affection of two amazing parents: my mother—who believed that Cleanliness was *before* Godliness—and my father—who believed in anything my mother believed in. In the twenty years I spent at home I never saw my father win an argument with my mother. He never even came in second. To this day he feels a great kinship with the American Indian.

Like many immigrants, my father came to the New World expecting to find gold in the streets. When he didn't, he got mad. As fate would have it, he found thousands of other men just as disillusioned, and from this disillusionment organizations were born: Anarchist, Socialist, Zen Buddhist—whatever it was, they joined.

With the coming of the New Deal my father joined the Democrats. In our house we had two pictures on the kitchen wall. One was a colored print of Moses on the Mount and the other was a rotogravure of Franklin Delano Roosevelt, and until I was fourteen years old I didn't know who came first or who was more important.

My father also joined the Zionists, a membership he's kept up to the present time. I remember we used to have a little blue-and-white coin box labeled "Trees for Palestine," and even though we were on relief, he used to put a few pennies in it.

When things got really bad and we needed some little thing like food on the table, my father would take a butter knife and work his way out of the problem. He used to say, "There'll be a few less trees in Palestine, but we'll eat bread tonight." Not long ago I visited Israel. Whenever I saw a barren spot, I thought about my father with the butter knife in the coin box.

My mother ruled the roost with an iron hand. She could stun you with one punch from any position, and never miss. I have an older brother who never had a fight in his life—and he looks like Maxie Rosenbloom. My mother had a right hand that must have been twelve feet long. It could go around corners, over doors, under beds. My brothers used to say, "Nobody escapes the sting of the Green Hornet."

She was always trying to get my brothers to make something of themselves.

"Why don't you go out and learn a trade?" she'd ask them. "Then, at least I'll know what kind of work you're out of."

I was the youngest and my mother would lecture me, using an index finger as a drill, boring right into the stomach.

"Are you going to behave?" she'd yell, turning the finger.

I am the only fellow I know with two navels. It has had a lot of advantages, of course. When I was in the army, I was able to carry two flags in a parade.

Actually, the story of my kind of boyhood has already been told. From early youth on, my life read like *Act One* (and why should *I* try to describe it when my friend, the late Moss Hart did it so well?).

❧ ❧ ❧

Jeanette and I were married in February, 1947, and we had the usual wedding—thirty couples from my side and fifty couples from hers (her mother was picking up the tab).

The big dream of my life and, I thought, of Jeanette's was to get away from our families, find a nice apartment, and set up housekeeping. I didn't want to live with her mother and there was no room for Jeanette to live with my family. We didn't have any say in it anyway because it turned out that our mothers were determined we weren't going to live with either of them. They got together and found us an apartment in an old renovated brownstone building designed, I believe, by the Collier brothers.

I thought our apartment was wonderful. In fact, anything would have been an improvement over the sixth of the bed that I shared at home with my brothers and the man nobody knew. I began to think I really had it made. We paid thirty dollars a month for the apartment, and it's the only place I ever lived where I didn't think I was being overcharged. We had a lot of luxuries. There was a toilet in the apartment, instead of in the hall. We had a dumbwaiter, too, so I didn't have to carry out the garbage. Actually, when I lived at home my brothers and I used to throw the garbage out the windows. The world was our yard. Our philosophy was: "Wherever we go, we throw."

Now all that was behind me. I was a newlywed with a wife, responsibilities, and an apartment of my own. This dream palace consisted of a kitchen, a bathroom, and two other rooms which could be used interchangeably as living room or bedroom. We never knew which was intended for which.

My wife's mother gave us living-room furniture as a wedding present. It was a secondhand set which she bought from a band of gypsies. We had beaded curtains between the two nonutility rooms and if you went through them too fast, you strangled yourself.

Our finest piece of furniture was a horsehair sofa. Unlike the imitations you see today, ours was made from the real thing. I can still hear my wife say, "Don't sit on the sofa. I just combed it."

Because my wife's mother had given us the furniture, my mother gave us an accessory—a genuine imitation mother-of-pearl comb and brush set. And my father donated his greatest treasure: an autographed program of a debate between Morris Hillquit and Emma Goldman at Irving Palace.

Since it was so difficult to decide which room should

be the living room and which the bedroom, my wife frequently changed them around without telling me. I'd come home late at night after working in a club, and feel my way around in the dark, trying to remember which room was which. It was the usual thing for me to end up sleeping on a lamp table or across a chair. I used to plead with Jeanette to leave a note on the front door if she changed the furniture around because I was killing myself every night. She solved the problem in her own way. For my birthday she bought me a pair of basketball shin guards.

The bathroom in the apartment was quite small. I think it was a made-over broom closet, and the toilet was placed at an angle in the corner which made it a little difficult for one to relax. You always had the feeling that anything accomplished there was not quite definite.

Directly above the toilet was a little wire clothes dryer on a pulley. You brought it down, put the wet clothes on it, and then pulled the dryer up to the ceiling. Consequently, whenever Jeanette had done the washing and I used the toilet, I always had the sensation that it was raining. It was not an unusual sight in our apartment to see someone headed for the bathroom carrying an umbrella.

Eventually, of course, the bathroom became the conversation piece in our apartment. It was talked about more than the horsehair sofa. I used to invite friends up just to go to the bathroom, because it was always good for a laugh.

When we moved into the apartment, we brought along four things, according to custom: Sugar—so that life would be sweet; Candles—for light in our lives; Salt—for the pungency of our spirits; and Bread—for the mainstay of our existence. As custom dictated, we broke the bread, dipped it in the salt, and ate. This turned out to be the only kind of meal I had for six months because, like most brides, Jeanette couldn't cook very well.

The first meal she finally fixed for me was lamb chops and raw carrot sticks, and I made the mistake of complimenting her. For the next few months that's all I ate. I tried to explain to her that a steak was prepared the same way, but she didn't want to take any chances. She was going good with lamb chops.

After that I became the cook in self-defense, and I've never eaten lamb chops since. In fact, when I go to a county fair I like to kick the sheep every once in a while when nobody's looking. If I hadn't learned to cook, this girl would be at the lamb chops yet. She can't even boil water today without making the process seem like the activity at Cape Canaveral. In case you're wondering why I married her—don't. You see, she looks better than she cooks.

Eventually, of course, that apartment became too lowly for my wife's tastes. Every time I got a raise, she went apartment hunting. She finally found what she was looking for on Fifth Avenue, within walking distance of Bergdorf Goodman and Saks. We had arrived.

The new apartment overlooked Central Park. It had an elevator, a doorman, and the biggest bathroom you ever saw. That bathroom became a symbol to my wife, but I was never really comfortable in it unless it was raining.

I could have stayed contentedly on in that apartment for a long time—but Jeanette had other plans for me. The ranch house in the suburbs, I found out, was just the first step. Beyond it loomed the shadow of a costlier, bigger house.

[3] HARRY K. THAW, You Shot the Wrong Architect!

CURRIER & IVES COULDN'T HAVE DONE BETTER. It was an old-fashioned country-style snow with drifts three and four feet high and enough wind to turn a paleface into a redskin. In place of the white rolling fields and frozen ponds in the old lithographs, the suburban houses stood —their split-level roofs and glassy gables shaggy with snow. Some cheerful genius was giving the morning television news roundup: ". . . It's a c-o-l-d morning, so bundle up out there," he burbled, ". . . schools in the area are closed . . . motorists are warned that driving conditions are hazardous." He smiled toothily

33

and continued with the weather report, ". . . the record snowfall is expected to keep coming throughout today and tonight, with winds up to 15 miles per hour, and drifting." Considering my luck, it figured. This was the day we were moving into our second house in the suburbs.

The moving men were supposed to arrive at the old house at 8 A.M. It was 9:30 when they telephoned that their truck had skidded off the icy highway and into a drift, and it was 11 before the doorbell finally rang and my wife Jeanette let them in—six guys who looked as though lunch break had just been called on *The Untouchables* set.

We arranged to meet the movers at the new address and Jeanette and I waded out to our car to drive over there. Our two sons, Bobby and Andy, were parked for the day with friends.

Seeing what kind of weather we were having, I was dressed accordingly. I had on long underwear, three pair of socks, a one-piece corduroy suit, a sweater I bought in Switzerland and thought I'd never use, and a trench coat I got from the wardrobe department of Warner Brothers some years ago. That coat, incidentally, is the only thing I have to show for two years at Warner's.

We crawled along at twenty miles an hour, the car heater sending out warm blasts of air and lulling us with the heat. Jeanette and I were quiet, both lost in thought. It occurred to me that I'd certainly moved up in the world—all the way from a miserable four-room cold-water flat on the lower East Side of Manhattan to a monstrous twenty-room English manor house on the North Shore of Long Island.

Of course there were steps in between: a spacious and comfortable apartment overlooking Central Park, and the little suburban house we were now moving out of. Ever since 1958 when I was presented to Queen Elizabeth and Prince Philip of England, Jeanette had wondered how we could go on living in our seven-room California ranch-type house (which she bought after I was presented to Governor Earl Warren in 1951). Thank God I never told her about the time I met Tonto.

In her search for a manor house, she had been conniving with a real-estate agent for a long time, but it was several months before *I* found out about it. By that time she already had the house picked out. It was a beautiful summer day when I was finally let in on the news. She had suggested we go for a drive. "It's so lovely today, Alan, let's just get out of the house and see some of the countryside." I was agreeable—and innocent. I even let her give me directions. There was one strange thing: almost as soon as we were out of the driveway, she started humming snatches of "Rule, Britannia." With my unique insight into the way women behave, I thought she was leading up to suggesting a trip to Europe.

35

We were driving peacefully along when all of a sudden Jeanette said, "Now there's a magnificent house, Alan. Let's go in and see it."

"Look, Jeanette," I told her, "you just don't go walking into any house you see."

"Wouldn't you like to see it?" she asked me.

"Sure, and I'd like to see the inside of the White House, too, but you just don't walk in on the President."

"Let's go in," she urged, "come on."

"I don't want to go in."

"It doesn't hurt to look," she said.

The house was half-timbered with turrets and spires canting out at alarming angles. There were leaded glass windows, ivy-choked walls, and a front door—in the shape of a Gothic arch—that must have been twelve feet high. Right over the door was a basketball hoop, which I found out later was a sneaky device added on by the real-estate agent at my wife's suggestion to prove to me that this was a good house for kids.

When I rang the bell I had a strange feeling that Gale Sondergaard would answer the door. Instead it was opened by a short, fat, jolly-looking man with a red face. He turned out to be the real-estate agent, and I later found out that the red face came from embarrassment.

"You're right on time, Mrs. King," he announced, beaming.

I looked at my wife. "We just *happened* to drive by, Jeanette?"

"Alan, we're just looking," she said.

Now my wife is a very famous looker. One day she went window shopping and she came home with seven windows.

We had a tour of the house and, after seeing the outside, the inside was just about what I expected. Here, I feel sure, was where they filmed all the old movies of C. Aubrey Smith sitting around discussing the latest disturbance in the Khyber Pass.

We rode up to the third floor in an elevator, and I could have carried a piano upstairs by one leg faster. I was curious about the elevator. The real-estate agent explained that the original owner had it installed because he had a cardiac condition which, I figured, probably developed when he saw his tax bills.

"The elevator's great, isn't it, Alan?" Jeanette asked. "It's a conversation piece."

"What do I need an elevator for?" I asked her.

"Don't be silly, Alan," she said. "How many houses do you know of that have an elevator?"

"Every one on Central Park East, West, and South."

Just about then the elevator got stuck for twenty minutes between floors and we got to know each other very well. I guess this is what they mean by "togetherness."

The top floor, when we finally made it, was cut up into eleven cubbyhole bedrooms, reminiscent of where the Christians are buried in Rome.

"Alan, we don't have to use these rooms," my wife

explained. "We can close up the third floor or use it just for storage."

As we creaked down to the second floor, she had an idea for the elevator, too. "Alan, if you're really sure you wouldn't want to use it, we could make a planter out of it," she told me.

The second floor had about eight rooms, a few fireplaces, and five bathrooms that must have pioneered the plumbing industry. There were Victorian washstands with floral pitchers to match, a couple of ancient, raised bathtubs, and the pull chains for the toilets were covered in braid ending in big embroidered plaques that read, "Lest We Forget."

"Why do we need eight bedrooms?" I asked, and before Jeanette could beat me to it, I answered myself, "I know. So we can close them off. You're right, Jeanette," I told her, "this is the house for me."

"But Alan, we can break through. We can make one room out of two."

"That will leave one room with two bathrooms," I told her.

"That would be a conversation piece, too," she said.

"Yeah," I agreed, "and if we get tired of it as a bedroom, we can make a planter out of it."

"A room with two bathrooms might be very interesting, Alan."

"Or," I continued, thinking out loud, "we'll make it as a room for your mother and father because they've had stomach trouble for years. Look Jeanette, if we eliminate the third floor and the elevator and if we make nine rooms into four big ones, we'll end up living in a seven-room house again."

"It'll be a different seven-room house," she said.

We decided to walk down to the main floor because I was afraid of getting the bends. I was almost prepared for the sight. One-fourth of the living room was a fieldstone fireplace with a big bronze plate in the breastworks. It showed three eighteenth-century drunks sitting around a table. There was a dog under the table and one of the drunks was just about to hand the dog a bottle. I sympathized with the whole scene. The house was getting to me.

There were two dining rooms—"the formal and the informal," the real-estate agent pointed out—which made it nice. You could dine in one and belch in the other. The formal dining room could hold a fifteen-foot table and seat fourteen or, if you were the sporting type, six official Brunswick bowling lanes.

"I would like you to notice some of the features in these rooms," the agent told us, "like this fine wood paneling." There was certainly a lot of it. I figured that probably the house was on the Diners' Club for termites.

The agent started to give my wife some of the history of the house and he got around to explaining the first owner's family crest. I wasn't too surprised when it turned out to be the plaque of the three drunks and the dog. He wound up his spiel by saying that the house needed only small repairs here and there.

"It will be a very simple thing to modernize, Mr. King," he told me. "Actually it's very sound. For the few changes you probably contemplate, it will cost very little to put the house in order."

All it would take, as far as I could see, was a J. Paul Getty's money and a Frank Lloyd Wright's imagination.

Finally I got a word in. "I'm sorry to break up this most interesting Grand Tour," I told him, "but we have to go."

"Well, what about it?" he asked.

"Yes, Alan, what about the house?" Jeanette put in.

"*Mere words,*" I told her, "couldn't do it justice."

This is a girl on whom sarcasm is lost. "Do you like it?" she wanted to know.

Now had I the persuasiveness of a debater or the oratory of a trial lawyer I might have found the perfect reply. Being Alan King from the lower East Side, I said, "It stinks!"

"Mr. King," said the agent, "I don't think you realize what a bargain the house really is. You're getting it from an ex-GI."

I think it was Benedict Arnold.

Of course in a few minutes it was all over. We were going to buy the house. In Jeanette's mind there had never been any question from the beginning. As we said goodbye to the agent and walked out to our car, I stopped in the middle of the driveway and turned back for another look. That's when I realized that Harry K. Thaw shot the wrong architect.

❋ ❋ ❋

"Alan, how are you going to get up the driveway?"

I came out of my reverie in a hurry. We were there. The wind seemed stronger now and the snow was drifting more. The driveway was about four feet under.

"You'll have to shovel a path up to the house," Jeanette decided.

I got the shovel out of the back of the car and started in. Halfway up the drive I thought to myself, "Oh boy, that elevator's gonna come in handy sooner than I thought."

About forty minutes later, when I was nearly to the front door, I had a better thought: they could just turn the elevator sideways, put handles on it, and bury me.

When we finally got inside, I discovered that the previous owner—a very frugal man (which he had to be, I guess, in order to own the house)—had figured out that at six P.M. of the day he moved, the last drop of oil would go through the pipes. We weren't due for a delivery until the next day, so Jeanette and I stomped around in the mausoleum trying to keep warm.

That was a memorable first day. You know how each house has its own peculiar sounds? Well, this house

41

was a whole special effects section in itself. The wind howled, beams squeaked, glass rattled, and someplace way off in the distance I could hear a toilet running. I wondered who hadn't forgot. Everything in the house was making noise except the heat—which was lying there dead.

By five o'clock that evening there was still no sign of the moving men. The phone at the old house had already been disconnected, so we couldn't call. By six Jeanette was frantic. Her idea was that I should go back to our old house and find out what happened. We had a short, uneventful argument about that—it was my day to lose anyway. There was no sign of the movers at the old house, just some empty beer cans and a few broken records. I could see what kind of an afternoon they'd had.

It was nearly midnight when they finally showed up —jolly, gay, and full of spirits—about a fifth apiece. I nudged Jeanette. "Let's not get mad," I whispered. "Let's get the furniture in the house. *Then* we'll get mad."

The foreman made it to the entrance hall, stopped dead, and began heaving and jerking around. It took some minutes for me to discover that he was dissolved in helpless mirth.

"Hey, fellas," he rasped out, holding his sides as he staggered back against the wall for support, "come on in and get a load of this place."

The others dropped a couple of packing cases that

tinkled and crashed pleasantly, and rushed inside. In varying degrees they went through the same performance.

At the twelve dollars an hour I was paying them, and at twelve o'clock at night, I felt, somehow, that I had the right to ask them where the hell they'd been. The foreman, who spoke with the moral support of Jimmy Hoffa, looked aggrieved, "Hey," he said, accusingly, "you hadda lotta stuff in the other house." He acted as though we'd borrowed furniture from the neighbors just to make his life miserable.

He turned to Jeanette, "How about makin' a little black coffee to warm up?"

"Yeah," I said, "and while you're drinking it to warm up, maybe you'll sober up."

"Hey, guys," he called to the others, "he's funnier than on television."

"Will you *just* get the furniture in?" I asked him.

When they started carrying it in, I noticed something new. When they'd picked it up, the furniture was modern. The time lapse and their handling had made it genuine antique.

Jeanette, meanwhile, instead of just being satisfied to get the furniture in, had started to decorate at the front door. This made the moving men very happy. She had them move the same sofa to six different positions in the living room. "Look," I told her, "let's get everything in the house. *Then* we'll move it."

She stared at me as though I was crazy. "No," she

said, "let's get it right while we've got the moving men."

"At these prices," I told her, "you probably couldn't get these guys to leave. I think they have adopted us."

But at twenty minutes past three the truck was empty and the house was a mess. When the movers had finally gone I splintered up a packing case to build a fire. Now there are seven fireplaces in this house, not one of which had apparently been used in years. I opened the draft in the living-room fireplace and immediately collected three dead squirrels, a couple of decomposed birds, and the tattered remains of what looked like a red suit. While I was still mulling it over, Jeanette gave me a nasty look. "And you told the kids he didn't exist," she said accusingly.

When the fire got started, I lugged a couple of mattresses over in front of it. We stretched out, close to the warmth. Manhasset Bay, outside the rear living-room windows, was crusted over with ice, and the snow still fell, blotting out all but the nearest sounds and giving us a sense of isolation from the world.

"Oh, Alan," Jeanette said, sleepily, "I've never been so happy."

I looked over at her. There was a gentle smile on her face and the firelight was glinting on her dark hair. She reached out and put her hand over mine. "Alan, don't you think it was all worth while?" she asked me.

Here we were in the middle of a blizzard, lying on

hard mattresses on a cold floor, trying to keep warm before a miserable little fire.

"Yeah," I told her. "We certainly have come a long way from the cold-water flat."

[4] IRVING, We Gotta Green That Makes You Tingle?

THERE'S A CONTINUOUS ARGUMENT going on among suburban homeowners: Which is the better buy—a new house or an old one?

One man will argue for the new house—where all the appliances are up to date, the wiring is adequate, and the floors haven't yet had a chance to warp. "Why move into an old house," he'll ask, "and take on someone else's headache?"

47

Another man may refuse to look at new houses altogether. He wants an older house—with the landscaping already in, the property values firmly established, and the previous owners' improvements already there for his benefit.

Now having gone through the experience of buying both kinds, I consider myself somewhat of an expert on the problem. I really believed it was better to buy the old house, particularly as my wife kept saying, "Any changes we make will be minor." When we bought our English manor house there was "really nothing to do but move in," according to Jeanette.

That was *before* we moved in and Operation Bankruptcy began. I honestly believe that my wife is trying to clear up the unemployment situation all by herself.

We have so many workmen running around that I don't know why half of them are there. I think there's some kind of sign in the neighborhood, like the kind panhandlers in the 30's used to have, that shows them the way to a soft touch. Any out-of-work plumber or carpenter tries to get his share of my wealth. All he has to do is walk in and act as if we sent for him. We'd never know. Friday night at my house looks like the line in front of an Army paymaster.

The house is a mess. Guys are ripping up tiles, pulling out walls, plastering, painting, and decorating. But this is only *in between* the coffee breaks. We serve more coffee at our house than Horn & Hardart.

Among my hired help are three painters—Lou, Irving,

and Eddie. They did a vaudeville act until they found a lifetime of ease with me.

Lou is an ex-sailor who spent thirteen years in the Navy, and I can never understand a thing he says. If he goes upstairs to paint, he says he's going to the "upper deck." And if I want to find the other two, he says, "they're forward" or "they're aft." I had to buy a copy of *Jane's Fighting Ships* just to understand him. Of course painters today are not just house painters. They are artists and Lou spends most of *his* day entertaining my kids by making his tattoo wiggle.

Eddie is the paperhanger of the group, and the shop steward. In his first two days on the job, he organized everybody in the house and threatened to strike. Because of my upbringing and my father's tendency to join organizations, I find it hard not to be on his side. I don't think Eddie ever wanted to be a paperhanger but he heard that's how Hitler started.

Irving is the sensitive one. *He* never wanted to be a painter but Eddie is his idol. He thinks Eddie is the greatest guy since Eugene Victor Debs. Eddie accepts this homage from Irving, and insists on using him on every job. Sometimes I don't feel I'm getting enough benefit from their work because Irving sits out on the lawn all day. He can't stand the smell of paint.

Jeanette and the painters are at constant odds. Before a color is decided upon there are endless consultations. After the color is mixed and they are halfway through, she runs in and says, "It's all wrong." Usually

49

it takes about half a day before they settle the argument. The last row they had was about a particular shade of green, and believe me, the UN doesn't have debates like this.

They were painting our bedroom and were about one-third through when Jeanette came in.

"Well," she said, "it's all wrong."

"Whaddya mean 'all wrong,' lady?" asked Irving. "It's the green we just mixed for you, that you approved."

"It looked different in the can."

"Lady," said Eddie wearily, coming over, "what kinda green you want?"

Jeanette thought about it for a minute. "Well," she said, "a green that's cool. And minty. The kind of a green that makes you tingle."

There was an ominous silence. Then,

"Irving," said Eddie, with a perceptible edge on his voice, *"we gotta green that makes you tingle?"*

Now I'm paying them ten dollars an hour, and my wife is trying to get a vicarious thrill out of a can of paint. "Do you want to leave them alone and let them finish?" I pleaded.

Well, she kept it up. Irving finally had to leave the room. The paint fumes were beginning to make his eyes water again, so he went out to the lawn while the battle raged.

Finally Jeanette said, "You know what kind of green I want?"

"No," we all chorused.

"You remember that picture with Deborah Kerr and David Niven where she was standing on the dock waiting for his ship, and he was coming back from the war? He had amnesia, but he didn't really have amnesia. He wanted to find out if she was in love with him for his money or if she really loved him. Well!" She actually paused for breath. "She was wearing a brown beaver coat with a brown hat and she had a green feather in it. That's the color green I want."

"You're wrong, lady," said Lou, who had been following this whole recital closely, "it wasn't David Niven. It was Ronald Colman."

"It was David Niven," Jeanette insisted.

"You're both wrong," Eddie told them authoritatively, in his capacity as shop steward. "It was Cary Grant. And he was poor. She was the one with the money. She was waitin' for him at the airport and he really did have amnesia and didn't recognize her. He was now in love with his nurse."

"Who played the nurse?" Lou wanted to know.

"Marsha Hunt, doncha remember? And he finally gets rid of this amnesia business. He leaves Marsha Hunt and goes back to Deborah Kerr. They make up with her old man and Cary Grant takes over the steel mill."

"Ya sure?" asked Lou.

"Whaddya mean, sure. I saw the pitcha nine times."

51

"Well, don't leave me hanging here," I told him. "How did it end?"

"There's this big strike. The old man brings in the goons to break the strike and gets himself bumped off during the fight. Then Cary Grant, seeing the evils of management, gives the workers a big wage increase, better working conditions, and shorter hours, which reminds me—" Eddie paused and looked at his watch. "It's time for a coffee break."

We never did get the green we wanted—but we had a most entertaining morning.

A few days later I came downstairs to find two men (I'll give them the benefit of the doubt) running around with tape measures.

"And who, may I ask, are *you?*" I wanted to know.

"We're Feibish and Bowles of East 62nd Street. Decorators," they chorused, flying around the room. They were wearing rope-soled sandals and tight Italian pants, and I wish my wife was built like them.

I can't understand why everybody is so anxious to have a decorator. I have nothing against them, but just because they get *House Beautiful* ten days before we do, does this make them special?

Our mothers didn't have decorators. Pictures from the rotogravure section and furniture by gypsies—that was it, but it was comfortable and it was home. However, women today are different. Having a decorator ranks in importance right behind major surgery—it's a status symbol.

My wife likes to tell her friends, "I can't go shopping with you today. I'm going shopping with my decorator." This means she's allowed to walk into stores that have signs in the window, "To the Trade Only."

You can't get into one of these places unless you're with a decorator. I'm very curious about that. I'd like to know what these shops have got to hide. The furniture and the accessories must be just a front. Something's going on in the back room that you and I don't know about.

So far we've had six decorators in our house. No decoration, just decorators. When my wife started talking about decorators, it was obvious that I was going to need a friend at the Chase-Manhattan Bank. I have asked for so many loans in the past few months I feel like an underprivileged nation.

The first decorator we had was a woman. She took one look at the house and went into a trance as though she was getting through to the spirit world. After a while she said, "I see this house as an Oriental palace. We'll use lots of temple bells and cover the living areas in marble and tile.

"We'll toss silk cushions casually about on the floor, and I've seen the most magnificent gong you can buy."

Well, I paid her for the seance and let her go. It was obvious that the most magnificent gong I could buy was her.

After that we had a husband-and-wife team of decorators who fought all the time about what style the
furnishings should be. I used to hang around the house
just to listen to the battle. They both wanted period
furniture but they couldn't agree on the period. The
husband was touting for George III and the wife was
strong for Louis Quinze. They spent more time fighting than decorating. The way they carried on, you
would have thought the reputations of their best friends
were at stake. She called George III an idiot and he
called Louis Quinze a gilded fool, and eventually
they ended up leaving George and Louis out of it
completely. She called *him* an idiot and he called *her*
a gilded fool, which made it simpler all around.

Another decorator we briefly employed wasn't too
concerned about the style of the furnishings. He was a
nature lover. He liked the feeling of "green, growing
things in spiritual harmony with the out-of-doors."

His suggestion was that we attain this tropical state
by growing ivy all through the house. Before we got
rid of him we had ivy coming out of faucets, key-
holes, and cracks in the wall. But the day his employ-
ment ended was the afternoon I came home and found
he'd planted ivy in a chest of drawers. The ivy was
hanging out of the drawers and my socks and underwear were lying on the floor.

Now we have Feibish and Bowles (they *must* be
kidding). Every time you talk to them, they've always
just come back from Europe. They never go; they just

come back. For a while I found them very confusing. They kept saying, "Mrs. King," but they were talking to me. They're now at work rearranging the living room, and already there's trouble.

"Now the first thing we are going to do is put a lovely cocktail table here," they told us.

"What do you mean, 'a lovely cocktail table'?" I asked. "That's where my chair goes."

"What chair?"

"That chair."

"Oh! That!"

I said, "What's wrong with it?"

They looked at each other. "Well," said one of them, "in our new scheme of things, it just will not fit in."

"What do you mean, it won't 'fit in'? That's my favorite chair. That chair has known me for years. I'm the only guy who went into the army and took his own chair. That chair stays."

Now these fellows never talk directly to you, they always talk around you. So, of course, they turned to Jeanette.

"You promised you'd give us a free hand," one of them said, tearfully.

"I'll give you a free hand right across the mouth," I told him. "Now that chair stays."

"Can't you give it to any of your wife's poor relations?" he asked.

"The way you're spending money," I told him, "the only poor relation she has is me. The chair stays."

Bit by bit they are moving it out. They have a new routine. They keep moving the chair from room to room. Now they have it in the attic. And when they go up to the attic to make a playroom for the boys, the chair will probably end up in the elevator.

But actually I'm really enjoying it. I like having these two around. Now that the decorators have taken over the selection of paints, there's nothing more amusing than watching Lou, Irving, and Eddie discussing greens that make you tingle with Feibish and Bowles.

[5] Next Week, Our House

I've BEEN READING some alarming stories in the newspapers recently which seem to indicate that people are disappearing.

They're fleeing from the cities. Every night the highways are jammed with cars leaving town, but there's practically nobody on the lanes coming in.

They aren't watching television. Ratings have fallen off, "Westerns" are waning, and sponsors' products aren't moving off the shelves.

They aren't filling jobs. "Industry Search for Talent Grows Desperate" screams the headlines, and "Teacher Shortage Termed Critical" points up the plight.

Variety reports "Movies Sag," "Nightclubs KO'd," "B'way Sad: Show Biz Is No Biz."

Can't you just picture all these houses? The lights are burning, the food is cooking away on the stove, the dog is howling—and there's nobody home. It's like a space movie where people are disintegrated by rays from an alien planet.

It's an eerie thought all right, but if it's been worrying you, forget it. I know where everybody is. They're attending parties in the suburbs.

I call them Reciprocal Invitation Parties. You invite me, then I invite you and two others. Then they invite you and me and two more. You see how it works? I think that back in 1607 somebody in Jamestown, Virginia, gave the first party and it's just been mushrooming ever since. It's a Pyramid Club for parties. It's got to the point where soon someone will invite the immediate world.

The ridiculous thing about these parties is that there is absolutely no reason for them. That's why hostesses go to such lengths to give them names. They throw Masquerade Parties, and adult, supposedly normal people carry on like idiots. They have Going-to-Europe Parties, Coming-Back Parties, and Come-As-You-Are Parties. There's even a Do-It-Yourself Party. You buy

a Shelley Berman record, a five-dollar bottle of booze—
and what do you need a nightclub for?

The kind of party my wife gives most often is the Surprise Party. You see, I hate parties but she loves them—
so, rather than *ask* me if she can throw one, she calls
up everybody she knows, plus a few others, and says,
"Come early. It's a surprise party for Alan." And the
surprise is that I don't know a damned thing about it.

Because the suburban party has replaced almost
every other form of home entertainment (there are
only a few of us rugged individualists left, you know),
thinking people are up in arms. Psychiatrists, soci-
ologists, and educators deride it in their books; ministers denounce it from the pulpit; and reporters lam-
baste it in their papers. What they're all alarmed about
is something called the "Switch-Partners Party," and
let me go on record right now that I don't believe in
that kind of nonsense. Suburbanites are very moral
people. If anyone actually knows just where these
switch parties are going on, I wish he'd come to me
because I would like to move to that town just for
laughs.

The suburban parties I go to—whatever the hostesses'
reasons for giving them—are all alike and all tame. But
since everybody else has had a stab at it, I would like
to take this opportunity to let you in on what does go
on. The Alan King Guide to Suburban Parties or How
to Get Gassed in Five Minutes tells the *real* story. These
other reports are, unfortunately, highly exaggerated.

Now the first thing to remember is that every party is made up of the same basic ingredients: The Directions, The Tour of the House, The Drinks, The Man Who Propositions Everybody (otherwise known as The Bottom Pincher), The Party Food, The Stereophonic Sound, and The Bottom Pincher (The Man Who Propositions Everybody). There is also, of course, the fellow who is footing the bill for his own surprise party.

This unfortunate arrives home after an hour-and-a-half of fighting the crowds and the traffic. He's had a terrible day at the office; he's worn out from the commuting and, no matter how miserable his home life may be—at that moment he's looking forward to it.

Now he walks into the house. He gets no "Hello, how are you? What kind of day did you have?" Instead, he sees strangers all over the place, running around moving furniture, unfolding chairs, and hanging up decorations. He figures one of two things has happened: either he's in the wrong house or the American Legion has decided to hold their annual convention at his home.

Finally he gets his wife's attention. "Excuse me," he says politely. "I hate to interrupt this Olympic Meet, but I'd like to know what's going on, and I would also like to have my dinner."

"There's no time now," she tells him. "You can eat when the company comes."

"What company? I'm hungry. I haven't eaten all day."

She evades his question, ignores his complaint, and

begins immediately to order him around. Now—in my home—at this point I begin to get annoyed.

Normally I'm a pretty easygoing fellow. I don't really care if Jeanette plans a party without telling me. I don't object to the money she's spent for party food and drinks. And I don't even mind waiting to eat until the guests arrive. But being ignored and ordered around *I cannot stand!* When she starts treating me like an adjunct to the party—on tap, but not really necessary—I blow a fuse. Women, however, are all alike. They all do this. They lay down ground rules for The Behavior of Husbands Before the Guests Arrive—and there can't be a married man anywhere who hasn't heard them all.

1. "Don't sit on the sofa. I just puffed up the pillows."
2. "Stay off the carpets, the pile is up."
3. "Don't go in the bedroom. I want to keep it clean."
4. "Hurry up and take a shower—but don't use the towels."

So what happens? A man ends up dressing in a dark closet and all night long he walks around with a damp skin, blotting himself with a Kleenex.

Meanwhile . . . the guests are trying to follow their hostess' directions to the house. Even if you ever received good directions—which is unlikely—it would be virtually impossible to find these places in the suburbs.

61

Nobody lives on Eighth Avenue or 116th Street any more. Then, it was simple. You knew that Eighth Avenue came after Seventh Avenue, 116th Street was a block up from 115th Street, and Avenue B was the one beyond Avenue A. But I defy anyone to find a strange house in the suburbs and be right the first time.

Today they stick a street between two trees, and even the people who live on the street are not too sure of its name. Every one of these places is called something like Featherbed Road or Poinsettia Place, and someone I know found his thrill on Blueberry Hill.

Some hostesses have maps printed up, which they send to you. At the top of the map it says, "How to Get to Our House," and the landmarks you have to watch for are not the ones a man would use, like "Turn right at the Esso Station." Instead you have to be on the lookout for "this little dress shop right next to a large gold sign that says 'Antoine, Coiffures.'"

Even this is better than the directions you get by telephone. The hostess will ask, "Which do you prefer—the Tunnel or the Bridge?" Well, frankly, I'm not too crazy about either one. Then she'll say, "Now write this down. Have you got a pencil?" Normally, of course, I write with a quill.

"Are you ready?" she'll inquire. I make suitable reply. Having made the trip herself, she takes a long breath and expels it at the rate of about seven hundred words a minute:

"You take the Triborough Bridge into the Grand Central Parkway into the Expressway into the Van Wyck into the Cross Island Parkway into the Belt which becomes the Southern State Parkway then take Exit 4 not the first Exit 4 but the second Exit 4 into Northern Village Avenue to the second traffic light not the blinker are you getting this?"

I haven't even lowered the pencil to paper yet.

Then she says, "Make a left turn and watch it carefully because there's a sharp turn at the flower shop but don't stop there. Really, I don't need a thing. You'll see a broken tree that hangs down like this" (over the telephone, remember), "then after the tree there's another tree and then there's a telephone booth but keep on going. Then there's a police station and you get out and ask."

So the trip is predestined to be miserable from start to finish. You drive and your wife sits next to you with instructions which look like the Dead Sea Scrolls. Now I don't know about you, but I can usually drive on for nearly five minutes before my wife says, "Alan, you should have made a right turn there."

"No, it says a left turn."

"Yes, but your instructions were for coming and we're going."

"It's the same thing."

"No, Alan, I tell you—"

So you can imagine what kind of mood I'm in when we finally arrive. I'm not speaking to Jeanette, I'm sore at my hostess, and I'm wryly amused at the prospect of a thrilling party—it will obviously be a small one—my wife, my hostess, her husband, and myself—because nobody else is going to find this place.

When you pull into the right street, however, there are always twenty cars in front of yours and I know now how these other couples do it: they form into caravans and hire the scout from *Wagon Train.* There is never a vacant place to park. Everything else is all planned out, but nobody thinks about where you can put your car. So, of course, my wife always arrives at the party first and about half an hour later I show up, having finally found a spot six blocks away.

Now many of these parties are black-tie affairs, but you can always tell the hostess: she's in toreador pants. Everyone is expected to bring a gift and the hostess is expected to say the same thing: "You didn't have to." Will you please listen to me? You *had* to!

Of course Jeanette and I never unwrap the gifts we get at our parties. We just wait until we go to somebody else's house and give them back. We always mark them to avoid the embarrassment of giving them back to the same people who gave them to us.

Since there is never enough closet space in a suburban home, your hat and coat are taken from you and thrown on the bed. If you arrived first, the only way to get your coat is to be the last to leave, because otherwise there will be thirty coats on top of yours. One night I saw a woman go home in a bedspread. The first thing she grabbed off, she took.

The next step is always a tour of the house. Do you know what a thrill it is to be guided through seven rooms and to have the functions of each explained? "This is the bathroom," your hostess will proudly announce. From the reading material you always see assembled in there, you could easily mistake it for the library.

After the tour you assemble in the party area—living room, dining room, and den—lavishly decorated and furnished to include a Louis XIV breakfront, a magnificent Empire table, and thirty-seven folding chairs (Early Rental).

Here, you must be on your best behavior. Good manners are extremely important at the suburban party. You must be careful of everything and above all—of dirt. I'm doubly conscious of this because I'm a cigar smoker. In my own home, life is impossible; in someone else's home, it's unbearable. My wife is constantly afraid I'll embarrass her.

"Watch your ashes," she keeps saying to me. I advise her to watch her own ashes. Then she grabs my arm and whispers frantically, "What do you think you're doing?"

"I'm putting the ashes in the ash tray."

"That's not an ash tray; that's a candy dish."

So why the hell didn't they put some candy in it so I could identify it?

Generally I walk around with a cupped hand. I put the cigar ashes in my hand and then I fill up a pocket.

Once, after one of these parties, I sent out a suit to be cleaned. Now cleaners, as you probably know, go through your pockets. That's how they open up other stores. My cleaner had nothing to gain so he called me up.

"Mr. King," he said, "it's none of my business but we found a pocket full of ashes in that suit you sent us."

"I'm glad you called to remind me," I told him. "My uncle died three weeks ago and I wanted to keep the remains close to me." We never did business together again.

One man at the party always does get ashes on the rug. He grins embarrassedly and says, "It's good for the rug." Then he rubs it in. How good can it be for a white rug?

If you haven't been given a drink by the time that remark is made, it's because twenty more people have arrived on your heels and are still touring the house. Just remember that you are never supposed to be without a glass in your hand. Once you have it, your job is to keep emptying it as quickly as possible—once every fifteen or twenty minutes is about right to enable you to keep up with the rest of the guests. This is known as "social drinking" and I've discovered that suburbanites are the most "social" people on earth. The trick is to get drunk as fast as you can, so you have some excuse for the way you behave.

Personally, I don't drink much at suburban parties. I do my drinking at the country club which I joined for one particular reason: I like to drink in the afternoon. If you go to a bar in the afternoon and drink, you're a drunkard. But if you're at the country club, that makes you a sportsman.

After about an hour all the guests are gassed and The Man Who Propositions Everybody goes to work. He doesn't kiss his hostess on the cheek—he pinches her bottom. This is considered good sport and, after three martinis, in good taste.

Now the Bottom Pincher is usually easily recognized, even before he starts to work. The BP wears a plaid dinner jacket, a ruffled shirt and patent leather dancing pumps. He is usually going bald but he disguises it, or so he thinks, by the use of a No. 4 eyebrow pencil. He still tangoes of course, and he was the only man who stood in the line at the Rudolph Valentino funeral.

At about the time this fellow has gotten around to suggesting that somebody else's wife lunch with him in the city next Tuesday (she says: "Oh, I couldn't!" He says: "Aw, come on. I bet you don't have the guts."), the hostess announces that the buffet is ready.

This is an amazing array of forty-one different varieties of food. There are fish dips, mayonnaise dips, creamed cheese and chives dips, and then you get little broken crackers or potato chips with which to scoop up the dips. Everybody always seems to be sticking their hands in this mess. Now, normally, I don't condone this kind of thing, but after putting hot ashes in my hand all evening, it's a relief to put a hot hand in a cold dip.

The food is always in borrowed casseroles kept hot by cans of Sterno which, at the end of the evening, the BP will be drinking.

The buffet also always consists of unidentifiable objects. If you recognize one thing on the table, you get a prize. There are always chicken livers molded into the shape of a duck, and I feel I'm taking a life when I cut off a piece of that.

They serve food like elephant knees au gratin, grasshopper fricassee, and chicken gumbo, which is all thrown onto the same plate. Everyone looks at it and says, "Doesn't that look delicious!" In the army we made jokes about a plateful of food like that.

There are no tables, of course, where you can sit down and eat this food. Tables, I believe, are considered in very bad taste. You have knees. The hostess gives you the kind of napkins that don't slide off your knees but the food keeps sliding onto the floor and that same nut keeps saying, "It's good for the rug."

I get very busy during the course of the evening. Since I travel around a great deal without having to apologize for not being home, I am considered something of a free spirit. Three or four men usually sidle up to me at various intervals and ask me if it's really true about Marilyn Monroe. I've never met Miss Monroe, who is probably a very nice girl, and I'm usually so busy I haven't even heard the latest rumor. But they're always sure I have some special inside information.

Just about the time I'm feeling trapped on the subject of Miss Monroe, we're commanded to come listen to stereophonic sound. That's the big new thing in the suburbs. At every party you discover that the host has just had stereophonic sound installed with the tweeters and the woofers and the Warfield speakers and the Garard changer. And the host is always an authority. Here's a guy who can't find the horn on his car, but all of a sudden he's a stereophonic-sound expert.

He urges everybody to stand at the focal point in the room. This is rather difficult since there are sixty people in the room and one little check mark on the floor, indicating that this is where the engineer told him you must stand to get the full sound value.

While the hostess pushes and shoves the guests up to the mark, the host puts on the records. They are beautiful things like "Dentist Drills to Read By," "The Secret World of Sam Huff," which records a pro footballer's bones cracking while being tackled in a game. The hit of the evening is a recording of a 707 coming in for a landing at Idlewild airport. Everyone swears it sounds as though it was right in the living room. This is one record I don't need at my house. Living near Idlewild, I have a 707 coming in about every twenty minutes.

About three in the morning a child comes wandering in. The host and hostess are too busy entertaining to remember that they are also parents. The child stumbles sleepily around and all the guests who normally don't pay much attention to their own children begin carrying on about this one. "What can we get you, darling?" they solicitously inquire. All the kid wants is to go to the bathroom, but nobody thinks of that.

By four I've usually lost my hearing and my senses. I've got ptomaine poisoning and I can't wait to get out of the house. Just as we're leaving, the hostess invariably comes along and says, "Won't you take some food home? We'll only have to throw it away."

Now I didn't like it when it was fresh, but here I am —I came as a guest and I go home as a garbage collector.

As I'm dragging my wife out the door, she turns around, waves, and calls out gaily, "Don't forget, folks. Next week, our house."

Over my dead body.

[6] Are You a Good Husband?

NOT LONG AGO a national magazine came up with new statistics on an old problem: divorce rates for 1961 were among the highest in recorded history and, said the survey, they're expected to soar even higher in the next decade.

It's funny, isn't it, how a thing like this can grow? When I was a boy, divorce was unheard of. It was a subject that was never even discussed, especially by the people who had one. A divorced person was a little beyond the pale—not quite a social outcast, certainly not a member of the in-group. And yet, oddly enough, people then had the same kinds of problems that we have today. The difference is that *they* worked them out. Divorce was a luxury few people could afford.

Today, with a higher standard of living and more money to spend on luxuries, people don't wait to see if the marriage can be saved—they just go out and get a new one. Those who don't spend much of their time with a marriage counselor. He advises them on compatibility, shows them the way back to love, and helps them find spiritual harmony with themselves and others. He's an expert on all these problems because he's been divorced five times himself.

If you don't have the time to go to a marriage counselor, or if you're the thrifty type and won't spend the money on divorce, you still can get in on the fun. To find out just how miserable your marriage really is —take a test.

Tests are very important in our lives today. They tell us what kind of job we can handle, show up our ignorance, find out if we're nearsighted, and let us know if the marriage can be saved. Even your doctor puts you through a test to find out if you're really sick or just faking. He won't take your word for it. There are so

72

many different kinds of tests that, if this keeps up, we'll see the day when doctors won't issue death certificates any more—you'll have to take a test to prove it.

Many tests, like the marriage ones, can be taken right in your own home. They're available free in almost any monthly magazine under a number of titles. The one I just took is called "Are You a Good Husband?"

I wasn't planning to take this test at all. In fact, I didn't even know about it until it was too late. I came home after a tough day of rehearsals for a television show—tired, hungry, and upset. As I was sitting comfortably in the living room, enjoying the tranquillity of my home and relaxing with my first martini, my wife walked softly up behind me, bent swiftly down, and greeted me with an open magazine.

"All right, Alan," she said, "take the test."

I was understandably startled, I think. "Test?" I inquired incredulously. "What test? I've only had one martini. I'm not blowing up any balloon."

"I'm not talking about the sobriety test," Jeanette remarked, acidly. "This is a marriage test. I want to find out what kind of husband you are."

"Look," I told her, "we've been married for fifteen years. Play it smart. What you don't know, don't hurt."

She came around in front of me and I could see that she was good and mad. "You won't spend another night in this house until you take the test," she told me.

"What's got into you, Jeanette? Who bought the

73

clothes you wear? Who bought the car you drive? Who bought you this house?"

She said, "You take my test first. *Then* I'll take yours."

"Look, Jeanette, it's been a tough day. I've been very busy and I didn't have time to cram for this marriage exam."

"You're afraid to take it, aren't you?" she asked, with one of her I-knew-it-all-the-time smiles.

"What happens if I flunk? You gonna make me single?"

She stood there with tears starting in her eyes, tapping the magazine.

In a desperate try to keep the dam from busting, I gave in. "O.K. Let's have it. I'll take the test."

I looked at the list of questions—an assortment of ridiculous riddles dreamed up by some spinster psychologist who's got it in for all men because years ago some man wanted to ask for her hand in marriage but didn't want to take what came along with it. In the test you score ten points a question. If you pass, you're a liar and if you fail, you're a louse.

Of course all these tests are ridiculous. A man's got twelve kids and he's asked: "Are you compatible?" They want to know, "Do you bring your wife home candy and flowers?" "Do you love her more each day of marriage?" "Do you fill her life with little surprises?" I defy any man to pass one of these tests without cheating.

Now for the one I took:

Are you in a good mood when you come home?

Do you know what a man goes through in one day? First of all, he's got to *get* to his job. He either rides jammed in like a sardine on an unreliable transportation system, or he's a wishful thinker like me, and drives his car into the city. This experience has been known to set up my mood for the remainder of the day.

And, although the trip into the city is bad enough, coming home is even worse. You speed along the highways at two miles an hour, bumper-to-bumper, gas fumes hitting you in the face and some imbecile on the radio is giving traffic information: "The traffic on the Southern State Parkway is medium to moderate." Where the hell did he get 'medium to moderate,' I wonder? I haven't moved for an hour. Then, you hear, "This traffic report is coming from helicopters." Sure, up there it's medium to moderate, but down here, there's no moving.

Two hours later I walk up to the house and she's standing there—her hat and coat on—and her opening line is, "We're eating out. Take me someplace."

"Do you mind if I come in and wash up, or do you have a wash-and-dry pad I can use on the way to the restaurant?"

She also gives me one other kind of greeting when I come home. "Alan," she'll say, obviously tense and trying to keep her nerves under control, "go upstairs and give those kids a beating." But one thing at a time.

(For full particulars on how I cope with *that* one, see Chapter 13.)

Now do you see what kind of mood I'm in when I come home?

Do you compliment her cooking?

Cooking, because of all the frozen dinners, packaged mixes, and bottled sauces, is today a lost art. In my opinion you have to have something before you can lose it. Since the lamb chop days, my wife's culinary achievements have all gone downhill. She inherited her cooking talents from her mother who was the only woman I ever knew who could louse up Corn Flakes.

Do you know how exciting it is to come home to a frozen TV dinner which *my* wife doesn't even bother to defrost? She puts it on a stick and I eat it like a popsicle. When she sets the table for dinner I have a salad fork, dinner fork, spoon, and an ice pick. And her idea of a surprise dinner is to take the labels off the cans.

Because cooking has been made so simple, there is now a wealth of plug-in appliances to heat up all the easy-to-prepare foods. There are electric frypans, electric casseroles that keep the food warm right on the dining-room table, electric coffeepots, electric toasters, and electric grills. And then, of course, we have to eat in the kitchen because there's no more room on the dining-room table.

Actually I once tried to compliment my wife's cooking. I walked into the kitchen, took a deep breath, in-

haled the aroma, and said, "Mmm, that smells good."
She turned around and stared at me. "Thanks a lot,"
she said, "I'm burning the garbage."

Do you do things together?

Everybody talks about togetherness. It's the battle cry
of magazines, ministers, and, of course, our friends the
marriage counselors. The only people who don't believe
in it are women.

The modern woman is a joiner. My wife attends so
many meetings and belongs to so many organizations
that our home life is like two ships that pass in the
night.

Once or twice I've made the mistake of asking her
why she doesn't stay home once in a while. "I'm just
trying to improve myself," she'll say. "Life doesn't end
with marriage. I must find my proper place in the sun."
If that's the case, then I'd like to know why she is always running around at night.

She has a weekly schedule for all her activities.

Monday nights she attends PTA meetings. "I go to
these meetings so I can express myself," she says. She's
attended so many PTA meetings that my kids are becoming delinquents.

Tuesday nights she attends a modern dance class with
her friend Clara Alcorn, to whom I affectionately refer
as La Grande Clara, because she has a face and figure
just like General de Gaulle's.

Wednesday night the girls get together for what I

call "Character Assassination Night." They sit around and talk about anybody who didn't show up. Since no woman will ever admit that she gossips, they play cards, too. This is to keep their hands active while their mouths are going.

Thursday night is maid's night out. Thank God I have the baby sitter to talk to. This is the night my wife attends the Health Salon and it's very important. For the past three weeks she's been on the critical list at Vic Tanney's.

Friday night is the meeting of the Big Three—Seances, Voodoo, and Witchcraft. I can always tell when it's Friday because she starts calling me Bwana.

Saturday night we go to someone's house for a party (the details of that you've learned in Chapter 5). Sunday my wife stays home and that's the day we really do things together. We settle down, lean back, and put our feet up. Calm and serene, removed from the cares and demands of the workaday world, we practice Togetherness. We both watch the same television shows.

Do you share your experiences with her?

A good question, so let's just go on to the next one.

Do you compliment her beauty?

Women are very vain. My wife spends a good part of the day beautifying herself and I spend a good part of the day waiting for her. I don't understand what takes women so long. I wait until Jeanette has her hat and coat on, then I start to get dressed, and I beat her out the door.

She's a living TV commercial:

She wears a Playtex girdle, a Maidenform bra, and a suit from Robert Hall.

She bathes in Camay, she takes a "Tree of Life" facial, she uses Maybelline Magic Stick for her eyes, and Miss Clairol for her hair. (Now you all know what her hairdresser knows.)

Let the rest of the world compliment her beauty. I know what she really looks like.

Do you ask your wife for an accounting of every penny?

No, my wife's a very careful shopper. Before she buys anything she asks herself three questions: Is it worth the money? Do we really need it? and, Can Alan afford it? If the answer to all three questions is No—she buys it.

Department stores could not survive without my wife. She supports them generously, reads all their ads, attends all their sales. She's the reason so many stores moved out to the suburbs. They heard we were moving and they moved right along with us. Today, before they run a sale, they call up my wife and find out if she's available. Even their newspaper ads start, "Dear Mrs. King."

I suppose you've noticed that women always say, "I

don't have a thing to wear," and my wife is no exception. . . . I wish the young lady who's got seventy dresses in Jeanette's closet would come over and get them out. My wife will buy anything. Once, after an eight-hour shopping trip, the only thing she had to show for it was a wedding dress. "Why do you need a wedding dress?" I asked her. "We've been married for fifteen years." "For $18.50," she informed me, "it can hang in the closet."

I don't think that most women dress for their husbands at all. They dress for other women. It's a continuous battle between women to see who can look better-dressed, and, of course, you can always tell a successful man by looking at his wife. She's usually wearing it.

When my wife isn't spending money on clothes, she's spending it on running the household. One of the real pleasures in her day is asking me for money to run the house. Some mornings I leave home at 7:30 when she's still in bed. I tiptoe out and there she lies, peaceful and relaxed, the mother of my children. As I get to the front door, she yells, "DID YOU LEAVE ME MONEY?" Well, you know, it's just like someone running a nail across a blackboard.

She asks me for money for the week on Monday. I didn't decide how much she should have. She told me. She wants to run the house on a budget. That's Monday. Tuesday, it's all over.

I can always tell when she's broke. At breakfast, she'll say to me, "Would you like some French toast, darling?"

It's going to be the most expensive French toast I ever ate. The price keeps going up each week.

"You want to loan me five dollars?" she'll ask.

"What do you mean, *loan* you five dollars? Why? You going to get a job and pay me back?"

"You don't give me enough money to run the house," she'll whimper.

Now I give her enough money to run the House, the Senate, the Supreme Court and the whole UN—but it never lasts through Monday. What she does with all that money is anybody's guess. Whenever I try to find out, she says, "Do you think it's easy raising two kids?" What does she do? Put them through college in one day?

Do you make an effort to curb annoying habits?

No, I don't have to make an effort. She takes that responsibility for me. I'm a cigar smoker and the only place I can smoke a cigar without getting into an argument with her is when I'm working. That's the reason the cigar has become a part of my TV personality. One night she was watching the show at home and when she saw me come out on stage with the cigar, she began opening up all the windows.

You'd think after fifteen years she'd be accustomed to my cigar smoking, but the minute I light up she starts. "Do you have to smoke that thing in here?"

"No," I tell her, "but it's twenty below zero and

there's a blizzard outside. You want me to walk the streets in that weather just to smoke my cigar?"

She just looks at me.

"Is it too much to ask to be allowed to smoke a cigar in my own home?"

"Yes," she says.

And that answer takes care of my annoying habits.

Are you a man your wife can be proud of?

I would like to think that I am. I have worked my way up in the world, I'm well-traveled, I have hobnobbed with people who are considered brilliantly successful. I dress well, my nails are neat, my manners socially correct. I'm witty and urbane in conversation, a peer among peers—but not to my wife.

"Isn't Sydney Johnson wonderful?" she'll say. "He cleans for his wife and he does all the shopping and cooking."

"Yes, and she works ten hours a day running her own business. Now do you want to change places?"

She ignores that. "Why can't you be more like Harry Berman? He's so affectionate. Millie says he always kisses the back of her neck."

Now I know Millie Berman and I think the real reason Harry kisses the back of her neck is because he can't stand the sight of her face.

Of course, you can see where we're heading. The last question is:

Are you still romantic?

What does it mean, *still?* My wife says I'm not romantic. She says I never do the "little things." I'm not tender. I don't make her feel cherished and protected. She may be right. Actually, I'm afraid to compliment her.

"Why don't you ever open up doors for me?" she'll ask. "Why don't you ever light my cigarette?"

"Because you don't smoke."

"Alan," she'll say, "don't change the subject."

If I tell her she looks slender, she says, "Oh? Did I look fat before?"

If I compliment her on a lovely dress, she says, "I've worn it three times already. You never noticed it before." So I can't win. There's nothing to do but agree with Jeanette. I guess I'm just not romantic—but am I a good husband? Listen to this:

When my wife added up the score, I got a 90 on the test. I *am* what you call "a good husband." Sure, I cheated on the test. The answers that you've just read are what I would have *liked* to put down, not what I actually did. But Jeanette's very happy. She has shown my test paper to everyone, and tells everybody she meets what a great husband I am. It's so easy when you know how.

[7]

Any women who may still be reading this book are kindly requested to skip this chapter. I didn't even put a title on it. It simply deals with the problems of the combustion engine, tells a little about the best way to fly-cast, and talks about the care and cleaning of hunting rifles. I think it would bore you women silly. It's really FOR MEN ONLY.

All right, men. Are we alone?

I realize that most of you fellows are rushed, harassed, and preoccupied with your jobs and your business problems. And with good cause—the market's up, the market's down, the government is asking for more money, the world situation is extremely critical, and in your firm you've probably got a brother-in-law who steals. But what can you do? It's *her* brother.

With all these problems on your mind, most of you must lack the time to deal with an even more crucial one: How to answer your wife in an argument.

Do you sit there seething inside, unable to utter the *bon mots* and pointed comebacks that can give you a firm upper hand and make you the envy of your fellow sufferers in the neighborhood? Despair no longer. I can help you find the way to more fluent repartee in just five minutes.

Years of research have convinced me that all women —in heat of battle—say exactly the same things. These gems of self-pity follow below. Beneath each one I have set down your own devastating reply, in eight emotion-charged sections. The beauty of it is that, no matter where she starts, you can answer, although personally I think you'll have more fun if she starts at the top and persists clear to the end.

Remember, this is one chapter of this book you can't ever be without. The minute she begins, turn to this page and follow my lead:

1. **W: *** "You don't appreciate me."

   YR: ** "WHAT'S TO APPRECIATE? WHAT DO YOU WANT ME TO DO—APPLAUD??? SHALL I CHEER EVERY TIME YOU DO SOMETHING FOR ME??? HOORAY! YOU WASHED MY SOCKS! RAH, RAH, RAH—YOU COOKED A MEAL! SIS BOOM BAH! YOU TOOK MY SHIRTS TO THE LAUNDRY."

   (With these remarks, you slow her up.)

2. **W:** "I'm nothing but a maid in this house."

   YR: "IF YOU WERE MY MAID, I'D HAVE FIRED YOU YEARS AGO."

   (Now you've got her puzzled.)

3. **W:** "To you, I'm just a piece of furniture."

   YR: "THEN YOU OUGHTA GET YOURSELF RE-UP-HOLSTERED."

   (You're dazzling her with your wit.)

4. **W:** "Why did I ever marry you?"

   YR: "THAT'S THE $64,000 QUESTION AND
   (She's stunned!)

* Wife
** Your Reply

THERE'S NOBODY TO HELP ME WITH THE
ANSWER."

5. W: "My mother told me not to marry you."
   YR: "THAT'S THE ONLY TIME I EVER AGREED
   WITH YOUR MOTHER."

   (You've really got her going now.)

6. W: "I'm going home to Mother."
   YR: "THAT'S THE THIRD BEDROOM IN THE REAR.
   SHE'S BEEN LIVING WITH US FOR FIVE YEARS,
   REMEMBER?"

   (If you're feeling cocky, hit her with the topper.)
   "YOU'VE GOT A SISTER LIVING IN PITTS-
   BURGH. THERE'S A NICE TRIP."

7. W: "You don't love me any more."
   YR: "WHAT ANY MORE?"

   (Now you move in for the kill.)

8. W: "I'll never talk to you again."
   (You look her straight in the eye and say—)
   YR: "PROMISES, PROMISES, PROMISES."

[8] MRS. SAGOFSKY, Meet the Suburban Supermarket

I BELIEVE everyone in the world has a favorite child-hood memory—the kind of recollection that is warming to the spirit and soothing to the mind. My favorite memory is of the neighborhood grocery store I frequented as a child on the lower East Side. It was run by a woman called Mrs. Sagofsky—a big, heavy person who always wore high-button shoes, a bulky sweater with a patch on one elbow, and a long white apron—a sort of land-locked Tugboat Annie.

Mrs. Sagofsky's store was the gathering place in our neighborhood. Here, during the depression, she dispensed advice along with credit, warmth and unflagging good humor along with the vegetables. In Mrs. Sagofsky's store, the smell of garlic mixed with the smell of salami and cheese. She had no proper refrigeration and no proper lighting. Her merchandise was not arranged in any kind of order, and the resultant clutter was more attractive and appetizing than any ordered design could be.

Mrs. Sagofsky was a retailer with the personal touch. We told her our problems, our hopes, and our secrets. She never refused credit to anyone and how she managed to keep the store going is a mystery indeed. My brothers and I used to go into Mrs. Sagofsky's and say, "Mom wants you to give us change of ten dollars," and one of us would hold out his hand. "Wait a minute," Mrs. Sagofsky would say. "Where's the ten?" "She'll give it to you Tuesday," we'd tell her, collect the money, and promptly buy groceries with it. She never turned us down, and she never found anything strange in the way we did business with her. She was truly a great lady.

Today, there are no more Mrs. Sagofskys. Our markets are blindingly lighted, freezingly cold, and electronically opened and closed. The odors of food have been sealed and boxed in, as though they were somehow offensive. We gaze at mile-high displays, select our meats through Cellophane packages, and stock up on one-minute meals.

If I sound unduly nostalgic for Mrs. Sagofsky, I am. I've just been shopping in a supermarket for my wife. And frankly, my experience—except for its ending—was so depressing that all I can do is joke about it.

My wife and I had finished—or so I thought—a little discussion about money. I knew the discussion was hopeless, so I dropped it. She, however, had just begun to fight.

"*You* go shopping," she told me. "*You* see how far a dollar goes."

Now I'd gone with her once or twice to a super-market, but I'd never been in one alone. When my wife goes by herself, she gets the bare necessities. The list she gave me was three feet long. I found out the reason for this: you see there's *her* money and there's *my* money and, of course, to a woman it's different money.

I was already out the door when she called me back. "As long as you're going shopping," she said, "take back a few bottles." That seemed reasonable—until she came staggering up from the basement with eighty-seven bottles. In fifteen years of marriage, I don't think she had ever taken a bottle back. She was waiting for me. On the one day I went shopping by myself, she decided to clean out the basement.

I drove to the supermarket where she always shops— and drove and drove and drove. These shopping centers have the most tremendous parking lots anyplace in the world, but there's never a place actually to park. You drive, and suddenly up ahead you see a vacant space. You prepare to pull in and there's always a Volkswagen or a baby Austin which had been blocked from view by the nine-foot-long tail fins of the car preceding it. These markets always have a big sign out front which reads, "Ample Parking." I've figured out that Irving Ample is the manager, and he's the only one who can get into the damned lot.

After parking three blocks away I had just the little problem remaining of getting the bottles to the store. I staggered down the street, balancing bottles and trying not to look like the nut I seemed. I neared the entrance of the supermarket and, of course, was spotted by the one wise guy who's always hanging around wherever you go. You know the type—he wears suspenders *and* a belt. Either he has no confidence in anything or he feels he has more to lose than anybody else.

My particular Nemesis was the gas station attendant from across the street.

"Hey, King," he bellowed, "where ya goin' with all the bottles?"

"I'm glad you asked," I bellowed back. "I'm opening up my own induction center."

I got to the entrance of the supermarket and came to a complete standstill. You know these electronic doors that open when you step up to the store? Well, I don't know what the one in your neighborhood is like but where I live, there's always a rotten kid using the electronic eye as a toy. There was one just ahead of me. He was jumping forward, then backward, and the door was obeying like a trained animal. I suddenly found myself fighting for my life.

"Look, kid," I pleaded. "Just give me a chance. Just let me in."

The clerk at the counter where I tried to give the bottles back just looked at me in a superior way.

"They're not ours," he told me.

"What do you mean, they're not yours?"

"Just that, Mac. They're *not* ours."

"Look," I argued, "of course they're yours. My wife doesn't shop anywhere else. They have to be yours."

He shook his head.

"Look," I said, "I don't want the deposit. Just let me put them down and rest for a few minutes."

He shook his head again. "They are definitely not ours," he repeated.

"I'll give *you* a nickel a bottle."

"W-e-l-l," he said. So that's how I got rid of the bottles.

It was a good thing I had my hands free. Have you ever tried to pry one of those supermarket baskets loose from the stack? I figured out that they take forty baskets at a time, put them in a vise, jam them together, and spot-weld them, because if you can pull a basket loose you get a prize. Because of this situation, everybody in the supermarket looks for a loose basket, and if you leave your basket for a minute, the next thing you know you'll see it going down the aisle in front of some woman who looks as though she could flatten you with one punch. When I did find a loose basket there was a kid asleep in it. I recognized him. He always sleeps in supermarket baskets. The other kids in the neighborhood call him "Waffle Face."

I cleared off a shelf and left him there and started my shopping. Now driving a supermarket basket is almost as dangerous as participating in the Indianapolis 400. These women drivers cut you off at every aisle. They use their baskets like weapons. They dart in and out, never signaling for the turn. There are more collisions in the supermarket than on the highways. When three or four women park together in the middle of an aisle there's traffic backed up behind them as far as the street.

One of the clerks who was arranging an eleven-foot display of cigarette cartons had "guide" written across the front of his white shirt.

"Could you tell me how to get to the vegetable department?" I asked him.

"Yeah," he said. "You go right on Central Avenue and you go down three blocks, make a left, and there you are."

Well, he wasn't kidding. The guy who figured out the design for supermarkets is the same guy who figured out the maze test for FBI agents. That's the one where the agents are put in a room partitioned with els, and only one of them leads to the outside. You can get lost easier in a supermarket than anyplace else. It's like the couple who broke up their marriage. They didn't fall out of love, they got separated in the supermarket.

I was lucky. It took me only about two hours of wrong turns to find the vegetables. Of course a crowd of women was there ahead of me. Have you ever watched a woman buy vegetables? They're all food testers. They touch everything. They press and poke and pick, and what's left after these scavengers get through is just miserable. They always want everything from the bottom of the bin.

I can just picture the frustration of the guy who waits on them and weighs up the food. He goes to work about seven in the morning and from then until six at night, all he hears is: "Trim this, weigh that, cut these, give me those. No, not that. It's too green." I'll bet if his wife says "Good evening" when he gets home at night, he goes over and hits her right in the mouth.

With a little deft thievery, I managed to get some fairly good-looking vegetables out of the cart of the woman next to me, and then I walked a couple of miles to the dairy products counter, and another few miles to the cereals section. There was one amusing thing along the way. At the back of the store there was a big sign saying, "We Deliver, Too." Right underneath was an infant in a baby carriage.

Of course you know that today these stores have every kind of service. They have nurses. Did you know that? They're in white uniforms standing around the place where the free food samples are given out. In my opinion, it's a little risky to sample food in any place where they have to employ nurses to watch how it affects you.

Like free foods, I think cereals are a little chancy today. Nobody bothers any more with what the cereal tastes like—which ought to be the first consideration. They just buy it for the box tops. Their children collect the tops and, if they send in five box tops plus fifty cents to the cereal companies, they get valuable toys like a plastic clown that costs the cereal companies a penny for every 1,000, or a picture of a baseball player that costs even less. I saw one little boy in the cereals section—a cute little fellow walking around with a penknife, collecting his own box tops the easy way.

This kind of petty thievery goes on all the time in the supermarkets. I know one woman who gets ten dollars more groceries than she pays for, because when she gets home she says to her kids, "Now empty your pockets."

It took me some time to get up to the check-out counters, and what an experience I had there. The line at the check-out counter is like the window at the post office. You stand in line and just as your turn comes up, they close the window. Well, it works the same way in the supermarket. Just as I arrived, the checker put up a sign that read, "Next Counter, Please."

I figured the express line would be the fastest so I got over there. Of course, I was new at shopping by myself. I found out if you have all day to spend, you get on the express line because that's always the one that moves the slowest.

As I was waiting for the three people ahead of me to be finished, a little old lady walked up.

"Excuse me," she said, "I just have this one package. Do you mind if I go through?"

"Not at all," I told her, gallantly maneuvering backwards and sidewards with my basket to let her pass.

Five minutes later a little old lady came up. "Pardon me," she said, "but I just have one package. Could I go through?"

"Certainly, madam," I told her and went through the same routine with the basket as before.

When it happened the third time I took a good look. It was the same little old lady. This was the way she shopped. She bought one at a time and she got out before anybody else.

When I finally made it up to the checker, I was in a rage. He was checking along, chewing gum, and ogling the girl checker at the next counter. All of a sudden he stopped making the tattoo on the cash register keys and said, "You've only got one can of green beans. They're two for 29."

Now everything in a supermarket is always 2/29.

"I only want one can," I told him.

"Yeh, but it's two for 29," he said.

"No," I told him. "You don't understand. I want just one."

97

He stared at me for a minute. "Com'on," he said. "Be a sport. Take two."

"Look," I told him, "I don't want two. Just the one."

"But it's 2 for— Oh, well," he said, "it's your business. That's 15 cents."

"What do you mean, 15 cents?" I asked him. "If it's two for 29, how can it be one for 15? I want just one, remember?"

"I know, bud," he said, "and that's 15 cents."

"I'll take the one for 14 cents."

He looked hard at me, and then he grinned embarrassedly. "Com'on now, will you stop? It's 2 for 29 and one for 15."

"Give the one for 15 to somebody else," I told him. "I want the one that costs 14 cents."

"There ain't one that costs 14 cents, Mister."

"Look, kid," I told him. "There has to be. If it's 2 for 29, then one can costs 14 cents and the other can costs 15 cents. I'll take the cheap one."

"Mister," he said, almost in tears, "you got to be kidding."

"Why?"

"*Why?*" He gulped a few times. "Well, can't you see? I mean— Aw, look, Mister, cut out the razz."

"No razz," I said. "Just give me the 14-cent can of beans and I'll be on my way."

Well, I had this kid crazy. He called over the assistant manager and the manager to explain it to me. Of course I lost this colossal battle. I expected to.

I had to take the 15-cent can, but it was worth the extra penny to see these guys trying to tell me *why*. I advise you men to try it sometime when you're shopping. It cheers up your whole day.

I pushed my basket out to the car and started packing away the grocery sacks. After all this—what did I have? I had finger-printed vegetables, sour milk, melted margarine, spoiled meat, and runny frozen foods, but I was happy. That experience at the check-out counter had put me in a fine mood.

I took the basket back to the supermarket. You have to do that, you know. There's a Federal fine for cart-napping. I think it comes under the Lindbergh law. On my way I passed a woman with a basket piled high with food packages. They almost obscured her small child who was sitting in the center of the pile. The kid had obviously had himself quite a time. He'd opened boxes, taken off soap wrappers, and peeled all the bananas. He had a Super Economy Giant-Sized box of cereal ripped open and was trying—in the midst of all the other groceries—to get the box over his head. It was a tough job, and he was screaming his head off.

Still riding high on the glow of my encounter with the check-out clerk, I stopped the woman.

"Lady," I said, happily, pointing to the basket, "your Corn Flakes are crying!"

[9] The Big Birthday Party Rumble

HAVE YOU EVER HAD THE FEELING that something which has happened to you was predestined? That this one circumstance of life could never have been avoided, never have been changed in any particular?

For example: when you yell at the kids, do you seem to hear a faint, ghostly voice, echoing back to your childhood—a voice that whispers menacingly, "Wait. Wait." It's happened to me. And the voice clearly belongs to my mother. She sounds the same way today.

Growing up, I found myself more and more aware that my mother possessed great supernatural powers. As a matter of fact, in her native Russia she was known as The Witch Doctor of Odessa.

Whenever I gave my mother any trouble, or annoyed her in any way, she'd lift her finger, seeming to stop all sound and motion. "Wait," she'd say softly, but with a veiled intimidation. "Wait. Someday you'll have children of your own." Everything she said came true.

Although I love my children dearly, I can't be angry with my neighbors who see them in a different light. My children are considered outlaws by other people. In fact, when they walk through the neighborhood you can hear parents off in the distance yelling, "They're coming! They're coming!" and they start pulling and grabbing their own kids in off the street. I suppose all Europe acted the same—awaiting the coming of Attila the Hun.

Every year on April 11th and November 19th my children become a year older. This is a biological fact which my wife can't seem to get over, and she attempts to celebrate the event each time with a pagan rite known as The Child's Birthday Party.

By now you know how *I* feel about parties; my wife knows how I feel about parties, and my children know how I feel about parties. So when either April 11th or November 19th rolls around, Jeanette is a little reluctant to come right to the point.

A few days before the last big event she walked into the living room where I was peacefully reading the paper.

"Alan," she said breathlessly, "do you know what next Thursday is?"

Being a fountainhead of knowledge, I replied, "The day the Treaty of Utrecht was signed in 1713."

"No, I mean besides that. It's a very important day in our lives."

"Your brother Murray's unit has been called up?"

"No. It's something to do with your son Andy."

"*His* unit has been called up. Is that close?"

"Oh, Alan," she sighed, "you never give me a direct answer."

"O.K.," I told her, "why don't you try asking me a direct question."

"All right. Isn't next Thursday your son Andy's birthday and isn't he going to be eight years old?"

"Yes."

"Well," said Jeanette, "I'm planning a big party."

"A party? Who'll come? All the kids hate him. Even his brother's not too crazy about him."

My wife ignores anything she doesn't want to hear.

"Now when shall we give it? Saturday or Sunday? Which day is best for you?"

"How about a week from Tuesday? I'll be in Pittsburgh."

Right away I got one of her favorite lines. "You're some father," she said, "you never spend enough time with your boys. You have to learn to be a pal to your sons."

A pal! My father had seven boys and one girl. His philosophy was that he didn't want his kids to be his pals. He said he had enough friends.

"When I had a birthday my father took my brothers and me to the candy store. We had a soda, my brothers hit me on the back—once for each year and once for good luck—and it took me a year to recuperate from the beating," I told her. "So let's forget about the party, Jeanette, because I honestly believe that giving a big party for a child is a waste of time and money."

She looked a little uneasy. "Well," she said, finally, "I don't know how I'm going to get back the invitations."

"Get back what invitations?"

"The ones I've already sent out for the party on Saturday."

"Oh? So the party's Saturday? And you've already sent out the invitations? Then what the hell were you asking my advice for?"

"You don't need to get so mad," she told me. "I invited you, too. Your invitation is in the mail."

"Thanks very much. That's already four cents you've squandered. Who else did you invite?"

"Oh," she said, "just a few people. Just the kids in the neighborhood, the kids in first grade, the kids in Sunday school, the kids in the old neighborhood, your nieces and nephews, my nieces and nephews, and the child from next door."

I looked at her in amazement. The "child from next door" isn't due for six more weeks. "Don't you know anybody else? We don't want him to feel lonely. How about running an ad in the paper?"

"Well," she said, "Susan's birthday is the day after Andy's, so I thought we'd make it a joint party, and so I sent about fifty invitations over to her mother so she can have her own guests."

Now Susan is a little girl in our old neighborhood and Andy is in love with her. If we had to have a birthday party, I was glad Susan was coming. Andy never bites anyone in front of her. He's on his best behavior.

I got my engraved invitation in the afternoon mail.

"Dear Freeloader," it read

"Hickory, Dickory, Dock,

The Party's at 2 o'clock.

You are invited and isn't that pleasant?

And don't forget to bring a present!"

If there's anything my kids need, it's a new toy. They're already stocked up like an arsenal. My oldest boy, Bobby, has thirty-seven pistols, forty-eight rifles, and three Thompson submachine guns. In case of an invasion he could hold out for a month. They even invited him to the disarmament conference. I could see that by the time the party was over, we'd have a bigger armed force than NATO.

My wife was worried about the entertainment for the party. "We've got to do something different, something memorable," she told me.

"Let's get a really good magician," I suggested. "Maybe he can make all the kids disappear."

"No," she said, "you don't understand, Alan. I want this party to be one of the most outstanding events of his life."

"Why don't you just charter a plane and fly him to Disneyland?" I asked, jokingly.

She said, "Alice did it last year."

"Alice did it last year?"

"Yes," she said. "I want to give my son something he'll remember for years. That's important to a child."

Well, all week long the preparations went on. The day of the party—the one day I needed all my strength—she got me out of bed at six in the morning.

"You've got to go shopping," she told me. "Here's the list. I've phoned for some of the things already, so they'll be waiting for you."

They weren't only waiting for me, they saw me coming. It took four trips with the station wagon just to bring back what she had ordered for the table.

I picked up paper cups, paper hats, paper plates,

paper straws, spoons, forks, favors, funny noses, masks, streamers, crepe paper, confetti, and place mats. I staggered in under centerpieces made of fruit and swans carved out of ice. I lugged forty gallons of ice cream into the kitchen and strained my back bringing in ten cases of soft drinks. A caterer made two big cakes—one for Andy, one for Susan—and about ninety small cakes, individually wrapped, for the guests to take home. I hired a trucker to pick up the extra tables and chairs and I made an extra trip into the city to buy balloons.

Did you ever blow up four hundred ballons? After the fiftieth you find yourself going up with it. I've been walking around with a collapsed lung ever since.

From six in the morning until five minutes of two, I didn't sit down at all. I hung crepe paper streamers, clusters of balloons, set up tables, unfolded chairs, wrote out place cards, put on place mats, set the tables, distributed paper hats, funny noses, masks, and the individual cakes at each place. Jeanette cleaned the house from top to bottom, wrapped presents, and shined the silver. Mrs. Kennedy doesn't give a state dinner like this.

At 1:55 zero hour was approaching. I dragged myself to a chair with a mounting sense of panic.

At 1:56, I told my wife: "I won't live through it."

1:57: "Let's post a quarantine sign on the front door. You draw all the shutters."

1:58: "Maybe we could catch a plane to Europe?" She shook her head.

1:59: "I can't take it," I told her. "I'm cracking up. I don't want it. NO. There'll be no party."

2:00: The doorbell rang. Jeanette and Andy raced each other to the door. In came this handsome kid in a snowy white shirt, gray flannel shorts and charcoal-colored knee socks. "Good afternoon, Mrs. King," he said, "my name is Bruce Belvin. I'm seven years old." He advanced cautiously toward me. "Good afternoon, sir," he said, "it's a pleasure to meet you."

Suddenly I felt much better. I began to relax. I even managed to grin at Jeanette. "It'll be fine," I told her. "This is a nice boy."

The kids came in individually, but put them all together and it's like guerrilla warfare. And in twenty minutes that's just what we had. There were maybe seventy kids in what was left of the house. About half of them were sticking pins in the balloons, shredding the crepe paper decorations, breaking lamps, smashing ash trays, and overturning tables.

To add to the confusion, toilets were flushing all over the house, seven mothers were screaming insults at one another, and Bruce Belvin had chocolate ice cream down the front of his filthy, rumpled shirt, his knee socks were down around his ankles, and he was busy crumbling up a hunk of cake and mashing it into some little girl's hair.

"Bruce," I muttered, weakly, "stop it."

"She called me a dirty rat," he said, reaching for more cake with his free hand.

Above the bedlam, I heard Jeanette's voice. "Children," she yelled, "CHILDREN!!! NOW HEAR THIS! Mr. King is going to make up some games. How about it, Alan."

"All right," I said, agreeably, "I'll close my eyes. I'm gonna count to ten and when I open them I WANT EVERYBODY OUT OF THE HOUSE."

At 3:30 P.M. I surveyed the battlefield. All the balloons and crepe paper had disappeared, but the windows were decorated with cake frosting which gave the place a kind of Christmasy effect, and the broken tables and lamps were strewn around in a pleasant, casual fashion. There was an ocean of gift wrappings on the floor and about two hundred dollars' worth of new toys scattered around.

The mob had left, but all the noise hadn't subsided. My son Andy was standing over a three-foot-long toy battleship. A little lifeboat attached to the big ship was smashed to bits.

"It's broken," he howled. "I wanna new one."

"Tomorrow," I told him, "tomorrow we'll see about a replacement."

"Today!" he yelled.

Jeanette sided with him. "Alan, after all it is his birthday," she said. "Take him down to the village toy store now and see if they've got another lifeboat."

Now an afternoon in a toy store can be very enlight-

109

ening. Toy manufacturing today is an amazing industry. I found out it's one of the largest and most prosperous businesses in the country. Most people think of
toymakers as pixies. You know, little white-haired men
with glasses, leather aprons, and candy-striped work-
shops. Well, don't let that image deceive you. These
guys have warehouses just for money. They pick your
pockets with puppets. They disguise their companies
with charming names like Tinny Toys for Tiny Tots,
the Busy Badger Toy Company, and Bambi Bambinos.
The stores that sell their products are equally cute and
coy.

The store we went to was called The Super Child's
Super Mart and I knew I wasn't going to like the place
the minute the salesman came up. You know that most
of these toy salesmen sound like Gabby Hayes or The
Old Scout Master, or Big Brother. This one was no
different.

"Hello there, Buckeroo," he boomed in his best
Dodge City accent. "Welcome to the corral. I see you
brought the old ranch foreman with you."

"Don't give me the old ranch foreman bit," I told him.
"I don't need the Disney dialogue. I'd just like to replace this lifeboat my son broke. My wife thinks the toy
came from your shop."

"Yep," he said, "it shore did. But we cain't replace
the lifeboat, skipper!"

"Don't skipper me," I told him. "Skipper him. Now
will you just tell me what I'm supposed to do?"

"Aye, aye, sir," he said. "Now hear this. You'll have to buy a new battleship."

"A new battleship! All I want to do is replace the life-boat."

"There's nothing I can do. They aren't sold separately." He looked over at Andy. "It's your ship, sailor," he said. "How's about it? Does she need to be scuttled? Shall we beach her and float another?"

"Yeh," said Andy. "I wanna new battleship! I wanna new battleship!"

"The government's not even building battleships," I told him with as much menace as I could muster. "They're obsolete."

The salesman had a new thought. "If the Captain here won't go for a new battleship, let's take him for a ride on this jet." He held up a model of a Boeing 707. "It's *only* $39.95."

Now that really gets me. This type of salesmanship is the result of television advertising. Every toy on television is *only* $39.95. Whenever I hear a commercial like that, it brings to mind some child living in a distressed area saying to his father, "Daddy, get me this toy. It's *only* $39.95." And the father's take-home pay for the week is *only* $39.95. On television, Art Linkletter advertises a doll. It's *only* $50, and the *only* one who can afford it is Art Linkletter.

I had seen this Boeing plane myself on television. It was zooming and looping and dropping bombs. Like most fathers, I bought the plane. Of course, when we got it home there was no zooming or looping or bomb-dropping. It just lay there like a lump. The only thing animated about that plane was the TV commercial advertising it. But, like the man said, it was *only* $39.95.

It was not long after we got home before Andy abandoned the plane and began playing with an old twenty-five-cent toy car I had picked up for him at an airport gift counter one night on my way home. He was happy as a lark and didn't even look at all the new stuff scattered all over the place. Some of it was very instructive.

He got a thing called The Human Skeleton. You're supposed to be able to assemble, remove, and replace all parts, and the instruction book claims to be written in easy-to-understand, everyday language. The first paragraph was very interesting. "Examine the skeletal system," it said, "which is made up of carpals, meta-carpals, phalanges, clavicles, etc., which form the structural frame, not unlike the vertebral column which is set upon a columnated system of defined, purposeful blocks." On the outside of the box, it said, "For age groups 4-to-8." I've got a friend who's been practicing medicine for twenty-seven years, and *he* doesn't know what this thing is all about.

Andy also got a toy called Mr. Machine. This is one of the most popular toys in America. You wind it up and it runs around the house, over the furniture, under the doors. It's like having another kid, and it's always good for an alibi. "Who broke the window?" you ask.

The kid says, "What are you looking at me for? Mr. Machine did it."

There was also a chemistry set among the presents, which I finally destroyed. Did you ever try to hit a kid with a chemistry set? You raise your hand, he raises a bottle, "We'll all go together."

My wife's brother gave Andy a wonderful toy—a disintegrating machine. We've lost three maids since the birthday party. We don't know what happened to them. We get up in the mornings and find an apron and a little dust on the kitchen floor.

Susan got a doll called Real Life Rosie which she left, by mistake, at our house. She's about 5 feet 1½ inches tall, costs about 100 dollars and she's supposed to do what all one-hundred-dollar dolls do. I'll tell you the truth, I hated to give up that doll. Susan got another doll called Betty Wetty. It functions as the name implies: the child changes the doll while you change the child.

A brief look backward has enabled me to come up with some approximate figures for the party:

> Profit in toys received: $ 200
> Damage to the house: $5,000

But at least I have something to look forward to. In another six months Bobby will have a birthday and I'll be hearing, "Alan, I want to give him a party."

I'm going to suggest we buy him two hundred dol-

lars' worth of toys, the four of us can go around breaking up three thousand dollars' worth of furniture and
accessories, and we'll save two thousand dollars on the
party.

The late W. C. Fields was once asked how he liked
children, and his answer was, "Fried."

The way I see it, he must have just come from a
children's birthday party.

[10] Status Seeker's Europe

I'M ALWAYS AMAZED by the number of people I meet who are anxious to go to Europe. You see, I'm a first-generation American, and my parents were anxious to get the hell out. But today if you haven't been to Europe, you're a nobody. Going to Europe is a status symbol. It's the thing to do.

115

This is so important in the suburbs that in some of the better neighborhoods the mortgage applications contain just two questions: 1. What is your collateral? and 2. Have you been to Europe? If the answer to the second question is No, you don't get the mortgage.

The suburbs today are divided into two classes: those who have been to Europe—and the Untouchables. The social leaders in each community are the people who *went* before *going* was popular. The only people you meet at their parties are those who have just come back from Europe, and the social climbers who are just about to go.

These upstarts have a bad time from everybody else in the neighborhood. They carry notebooks so they can write down all the helpful hints the people who have already been to Europe give them, and they sit at the feet of the social leaders and grovel. I know, because in my old neighborhood I was a social outcast. In the new neighborhood—having done the right thing and gone to Europe several times—I belong. As a matter of fact, Jeanette and I are the social leaders.

I've learned a great deal about this important position just by listening to my wife, and some of what I've learned I'd like to pass along to you.

For example: If you haven't been to Europe yet, you're probably planning to move into a brand-new neighborhood where your social drawbacks aren't already known. Now take my advice. Buy the new house, throw your furniture into it, lock the door, and get on a plane to Europe. You've got probably the only chance in your lifetime to be the first in your area to go abroad. What does it matter if everybody else is settled in by the time you get back? You'll be the social leader when you return and, out of respect, all your neighbors will come in and settle the place for you.

Those of you who aren't in such a serious position can't afford to relax either. It may become necessary for you to go abroad for a refresher course, just to keep up with everybody else. The leaders are the only lucky ones: they had to go just once—even if it was twenty years ago—but they had to be first.

As a leader your job is to deride the travel plans of everybody else, particularly social climbers making their first pilgrimage. You are supposed to make sure these inferior people have a miserable time from the minute they leave home. Here are three ways to do it:

1. *Be sympathetic.* When someone announces he's leaving for a first trip to England, stare at him a moment and then say kindly, "I'm sorry you won't see the old London—the one *before* the war. There weren't so many tourists then."

2. *Be helpful.* Offer to give him the name of your favorite European restaurant but fix it in such a way that he'll never get there. "You must try a great little restaurant," tell him. "I'll give you a note to the head-waiter. You won't be able to get in without it."

He, of course, will whip out his notebook, pencil at

117

the alert, and attend your every word. Now you pause, and look slightly embarrassed. "Oh, I forgot," you say, "you're going in August? They'll be closed. Everything in Europe is closed in August. It's the worst time to go."

3. *Be bilingual.* "You don't speak French?" you inquire, trying not to look sick. Then rally, and give him a big grin. "Well, no matter. So many French speak English. *Pourtant, c'est dommage.* You don't really get to know a country until you have some insight into the nuances of the language."

Now you simply keep applying variations of these three rules to anything he says about his plans. You can tell him (as Jeanette has done, for instance) that the hotel he's picked in Rome "is really quaint and filled with Americans, so you won't feel lonely at all." Then add, "Of course, if you're going to Europe just to be with Americans, you might as well stay at home, *n'est-ce pas?*

If he's planning to see a bullfight, tell him *"la fiesta brava* isn't like the old days." Remind him that the shaving of the horns (to make it a very "inside" thing) "has taken away the drama and the danger."

If he's going to France and not to Spain, casually mention that you think "the Louvre can't be truly appreciated without having seen the Prado also."

You see how it works? By being sympathetic, helpful, and bilingual, you'll make sure that he hates every minute of his trip. And, since he won't dare go any of the places you've lightly criticized, he'll never be in a position to dispute your opinions.

All of the above tactics may not work for you, but this is the way my wife carries on. To hear her talk, the people who write travel guides don't make a move without her. She's an authority on everything. Just the other night I heard her advising a neighbor about where to go. "Why don't you spend two weeks at Antibes, one week on the Costa Brava, and a weekend at San Remo?" she suggested. Now, I wonder if you realize that this is the same girl who, ten years ago, was looking for a nail at Coney Island to hang her bathing suit on?

Because a European trip is a prerequisite to success in the suburbs, I'd like to tell you something about the first trip we took. For you men who haven't been abroad yet, it'll show you what you can expect from your wives—and maybe *you* can figure out a way to avoid what I went through. It may also have the advantage of showing you what *not* to tell your neighbors about the trip when you get back.

Now before I became the leader, life—back in our old neighborhood—was impossible. We'd had vacations at the seaside, we'd camped out in the mountains, we'd been to Las Vegas—but socially we didn't belong. We'd never been to Europe.

Jeanette, of course, wasn't going to put up with this a minute longer than she had to. She kept after me night and day: "Alan, it doesn't look nice that we haven't been to Europe." One day she walked into a market and the clerk said, "There goes Mrs. King. She hasn't been to Europe." She came home and started packing that night.

That first trip was a memorable one. We are the only people I know of who actually went to Europe for spite because every time I asked my wife what kind of trip she wanted, she said, "The type of trip that when the neighbors hear about it, they'll drop dead."

She wanted to get to so many places in a month that we spent most of the time touching down at airports. We didn't have an opportunity to *see* many countries. We just gassed up and went on to the next.

The travel book we read was a big help in planning the trip. Under a section entitled, "What the Well-dressed Gentleman Air Traveler Should Take," there were twenty-two items of apparel. Things like extra shorts and socks, pajamas, a robe, a sweater, a dress shirt, and slippers. We boarded the plane with one hundred twenty pounds of luggage—one hundred eighteen pounds for her and two pounds for me. She gave me permission to take two wash-and-wear suits. One I wore and the other I carried rolled up in a flight bag. She figured that would be all I'd need. Of course we traveled so continuously that the suits never had a chance to dry, so I went all over Europe in a damp suit, wringing out the bottom of my cuffs as the water dripped down, and leaving a suspicious trail of small puddles in my wake.

The first city we hit was Lisbon which was just a refueling stop. The minute we touched down, she said, "Run out and send postcards." The plane hadn't even stopped rolling yet. "Look," I told her, "we're not gonna be here." "The neighbors won't know," she argued.

Her idea was to send as many postcards from as many different places as she possibly could, so all I had to show for a month's vacation was writer's cramp and an ink-stained finger.

Our first real stopover was in Spain. Jeanette decided this was one country we should visit because nobody else in the neighborhood had. We went to a charming little restaurant our first night in Madrid, looking for atmosphere—exotic Spanish food and flamenco music. As we walked in, we heard American rock 'n' roll, played by an Italian trio.

Since we couldn't speak the language we decided to order a little of everything on the menu, sort of like Chinese food. We figured we'd have eight or ten dishes and we'd taste everything and if we came up with two we liked, we'd be happy.

Most of the food was deep-fried in oil, which we weren't used to, but finally the waiter brought out what looked like little shoestring potatoes. Jeanette tasted these and said they were delicious, and she really started to eat. After she had downed half a plate-

121

ful, I figured it was safe to tell her the truth. "You're eating octopus," I told her—and she fainted dead away.

For the next three days she took just enough nourishment to survive. She'd drink a little soup, she'd have some tea and a roll, but nothing else. Every time she thought of the octopus, she went out of her mind.

Finally, I heard about the Casa Botin that Hemingway made so famous in *The Sun Also Rises*, and Jeanette decided that if Hemingway had eaten there, the restaurant would be bound to have something she would like. We arrived at Botin, a narrow, tiled little restaurant with wine cellars and old-fashioned roasting ovens, and I proceeded to order the specialty of the house—roast suckling pig.

Jeanette drank some wine and started to eat some salad and, for the first time, she was actually looking forward to a meal. In came the suckling pig, split down the middle, on a long baker's plank. The waiter put the part with the head in front of me, so Jeanette had a fine view of the other end, with its little scorched tail sticking up in the air—and she fainted dead away again. That was the end of our dining-out in Spain.

The next afternoon, before we left, I decided we should take in a bullfight. Jeanette didn't want to go. By this time her one desire was to get out as fast as possible, but I held out for the bullfight. Having read *Death in the Afternoon*, I considered myself an *aficionado*. We had good seats in the first row, directly behind the bullfighters in the *callejon*. One of them,

I noticed, began to show off a little in front of Jeanette. The more he showed off, the more I found myself rooting for the bull. He dedicated his last bull of the afternoon to my wife, and even *I* have to admit that he was very good. He cut an ear (the bull's)—which is like a prize you're granted for being good at your job (Spain is a pretty poor country, you know)—and he brought over the ear and presented it to my wife.

Now here's a girl who fainted at the sight of octopus and suckling pig, who didn't want to come to the bullfight, and who couldn't wait to get out of Spain. But there she was, standing up, bowing and smiling, and holding this dirty sawed-off ear in her hand—and *I* fainted dead away.

I was so anxious to get out of Spain that we ended up on an unscheduled airline where the passengers sat eleven abreast. A kid sitting next to me was practicing to be a mountain climber and he was all over me on the trip to Rome. I finally had to hit him just a little bit, not enough to injure him, you know, just enough to keep him quiet.

The door to the cockpit was open during the flight and the pilots had a big bottle of wine between them on the floor. They didn't have the guts to fly this plane sober. They took turns swigging out of the bottle and, after a while, they broke into song. They were singing "Three Coins in the Fountain," as we made our approach to Rome, and that's honestly where I thought we were going to end up.

We took a cab to the Excelsior Hotel and I didn't see Jeanette, except at a distance, for the next two days. She didn't even unpack. She sat downstairs drinking espresso and waiting for the stores to open. She shopped down one side of the street and then she shopped back up the other side. Rome, as you know, is famous for its shoes, and my wife bought forty pounds' worth. If she believed in reincarnation, she'd be all set. She could come back as a centipede. She'd spend down to the last lira she had, and then she'd take a taxi back to the Excelsior and ask the doorman for money. When she bought all the shoes that were available in Rome, she started in on the dresses.

I tried to interest her in other things besides shopping. Rome, the Eternal City, the land of the Caesars, Michelangelo, and the Catacombs—a city unparalleled culturally for twenty-five hundred years—lay before us. I wanted to see it all, and I wanted her to see it, too. Finally I got her to the Forum where Julius Caesar was supposed to have been assassinated. We looked out over the ancient and magnificent ruins and she turned to me and said, "Alan, do you see what happens when you let a neighborhood run down?"

While in the Eternal City we bought two extra suitcases to hold her purchases and it cost me two hundred dollars in postage to send home gifts. She bought gifts for people we didn't like, just to aggravate them. "Why are you spending all this money on people you hate?" I asked her. "To burn them up," she said. "It'll make them mad, you know, that we're here and they're there."

To thousands of people, Paris—our next stop—is a city of lights, wide boulevards, art treasures, and lovers strolling along the Seine—but to my wife it was just one big shopping center. She wouldn't see anything. She just bought.

Finally, I decided I had to do something. "This has got to stop, Jeanette," I told her. "You have to see something of this beautiful city. Now I've got an idea. You meet me at the Louvre today and we'll really have ourselves a wonderful afternoon." Her eyes got very bright. "Great," she said, "I'll be there. Oh, Alan, I can hardly wait."

That was the last I saw of her until early evening when she came back to the hotel boiling with rage. Now if I told a Tennessee mountain man to meet me at the Louvre in Paris, he would meet me at the museum, but Jeanette stood all afternoon in front of the Louvre Department Store. She couldn't understand why anybody would want to do anything else in Paris but go to shops.

One of the greatest attractions in Paris is the Eiffel Tower, affectionately referred to as General de Gaulle's erector set. According to my guidebook, it was built in 1889, formally inaugurated by Edward VII, Prince of Wales, and is the most universally famous of all Paris monuments. When I finally got her to go see that, she took one look at it and said, "What's it for?"

"What do you mean, what's it for?" I asked her. "It's been there for years. It's a symbol of Paris. It's just there."

"I can see that," she said. "But what's it for? What's the reason?"

"Well," I said, "they built it so they could put a red light on top of it so the airplanes wouldn't hit it." And that answer seemed to satisfy her completely.

Since we had the opportunity, I decided we should see some of the country, so I made up my mind to rent a car we could drive to the South of France. I met a fellow in the street and struck up a chance conversation with him. After we'd talked for a while, I said I was on my way to try and rent a car.

"Don't bother going farther," he said. "You meet me tonight at nine o'clock and I'll have a car for you. You can bring your wife, but make sure you're not followed." He gave me the address of our meeting place, a little winding street over in Montmartre.

When I told Jeanette, she was against the whole thing. She was sure we were going to be cheated. But that evening we arrived at the rendezvous to find the man waiting for us with a small French car, compact and sturdy-looking. I handed over the money we had agreed upon, and our friend left.

"Take a look at the motor, Alan," Jeanette suggested, knowingly. Now you understand that she doesn't even know where the steering wheel is, but all of a sudden she's a mechanic. I opened up the front of the car and,

126

of course, there was no motor. She was very happy. She thought she'd shown me up.

"All right, Jeanette. It's a foreign car. The motor's in the rear," I told her.

I opened up the back where the trunk usually is and, sure enough, there was no motor. It was the kind of car that you couldn't go anyplace in, but you had a lot of trunk space.

We did the only thing there was to do: we put our feet through and pedaled our way to the South of France. It was a pretty good trip. I figure I got about sixty miles per day out of my wife.

With all the money she had been spending on clothes, I decided we shouldn't go through agents and book expensive hotels, so we arrived in the South with no reservations. We made no reservations and we got no rooms—it was as simple as that. We ended up in one of those tents that the kids put up around Juan-les-Pins but it wasn't exactly satisfactory.

Eventually, by asking around I heard about a little place in Cannes where someone thought we could get in. I felt it looked a little suspicious when we went in, and my suspicions were right. The kindest way to describe it would be to say that it was a sort of French version of the YWCA, except that there the girls were allowed visitors.

I spent most of my time on the beach indulging in that great American tourist sport of watching these magnificent animals walk by in the Bikinis, consisting of two Band-Aids and a hockey puck. It really was unfair having to compare the mademoiselles of France with my madame. It was then that I realized I married a boy.

It didn't take long for the charms of France to pall on Jeanette in that atmosphere, so I wasn't too surprised one morning to come in from the beach and find her packing for England.

We really enjoyed London and I actually got her to see some of the places of interest. Everyplace she went, she carried a travel guide that gave descriptions of everything we saw. After each monument, castle, or building, there was a bunch of hieroglyphics like this: 3CCCBOA. Roughly translated, this means that you should spend at least three hours there, and the place is considered highly cultural. I thought BOA had something to do with the airline, but the explanation was that you should Beware of Other Americans.

We were in London just two days when The Big Jewel Robbery took place. When we left our hotel for dinner one night, Jeanette left a bracelet she had bought in Paris lying on a table in our room. When we came back, it wasn't there. It was "presumably burgled" as they say in England. Jeanette took the whole thing calmly. She lay down on the floor, kicked her feet, yelled, and carried on.

"Don't get excited," I told her. "We'll find it. If it was stolen, we'll get it back. In fact," I said, "we'll call Scotland Yard." I had seen so many movies where this kind of thing happened that I thought it was the thing to do.

Scotland Yard sent over an inspector and, had you called Central Casting, you couldn't have found a more perfect character for the role. This guy *was* Scotland Yard, complete with mackintosh, bowler, heavy walrus mustache, and umbrella.

He "interrogated" us, made some notes, and left. About four in the morning, the phone rang. I fumbled around in my sleep and finally picked it up, and a voice said, "Scotland Yard, heah."

Without even waiting for more, I woke up Jeanette.

"They've found it!" I yelled, jubilantly. "They've got the bracelet."

"Where did you find it?" I asked my caller.

"Well," he said, "we haven't actually *found* the bracelet, Mr. King. I've misplaced my umbrella. I wonder, did I leave it there?"

Despite all this, England has become my favorite European country. And I've grown to love London, its monuments, its clubs, and its shops. It's often been referred to as a Man's Town, but my wife will never let me find out. She keeps going with me.

Of course, you realize that the story of our first trip is not the story the neighbors heard when we got back. The way Jeanette tells it, you'd think we stayed with Grace and Rainier the one night we spent at Monte Carlo. "If she's such a good friend, why don't you invite her to the next B'nai B'rith luncheon?" a neighbor asked her. "She can't get a sitter," Jeanette replied.

Naturally in our new home, with this kind of start, it was nothing for her to become the social leader. She's made ten trips to Europe, and she even went to a 1958 Royal Command Performance in Glasgow where I did my suburban routine for Queen Elizabeth and Prince Philip. With her kind of record, no one in the neighborhood stands a chance.

This year, with all the expenses incurred with the new house, we're not going to Europe, and all the women in the neighborhood are trying to pay my wife back. Just last week somebody said to her, "You mean *you're* not going to Europe this year?"

"Oh, no," she said, very positively. "Spain is too depressing, Italy's overcrowded, and France is so bohemian."

Here's a girl who—in one sentence—just destroyed three countries. Her trick worked, though, because nobody else is going either. That gives her the time she needs to plan her next year's vacation. She's been around the world. Now she's looking for someplace else. I wonder if she's heard about this latest thing: you go down to Cape Canaveral, get into this rocket, and—

[11] SIR,
If You Dropped
Dead Tomorrow...

I READ RECENTLY that Americans are the most heavily insured people of any country in the world. This obviously makes insurance one of the biggest businesses we have—and one of the most prosperous. United States life insurance companies alone last year admitted assets of $120,576 *millions.* Yet, to hear the insurance companies tell it, nobody makes a nickel from insurance. It's pure charity—a share-the-wealth socialistic program. They're right. Whatever you give them, they spend.

Now the one thing that nobody really understands is insurance. It's like the law—and the lawyers and the insurance companies want to keep it that way, because the less you know about it, the bigger their income is.

They confuse you with legal and technical terms. An insurance salesman fixes you with a hypnotic stare and says, "Now in your occupational class, we can have the incontestability of the grace period on the basis of calculations made convertible for nonforfeitage of values, *unless* a waiver of payment of premiums falling due from the commencement of and during the disability is made, is that clear?"

All you want to know is: how much do you pay every month? And the salesman always comes back with, "My dear man. In insurance you *never* pay. You save. Why, it's like taking it from one pocket and putting it in another."

And that's exactly right. From your pocket into their pocket.

Perhaps you've noticed that some of the most beautiful and expensive commercial buildings in the country belong to insurance companies. Yet, according to their propaganda, they're always paying out to their insurees. Somebody's screwing up the books somewhere, because some of that money they're always paying out is sticking to the cash drawers at the home office. How else can they afford those impressive buildings?

They're handing out money for self-advertising, too. Everywhere you turn, there's an insurance ad. Now

insurance advertising is among the world's most interesting literature. The insurance companies work on the
theory that fear is the best basis for salesmanship.
They try to scare you to death.

How many times have you picked up a magazine,
opened it and read: "According to the statistics, four
thousand of you reading this advertisement right now
will not live out the week"?

Or, how about the ad that shows a family group—
loving mother, son, and daughter—and the headline
reads: "What If *You're* Not in the Picture?"

Of course, you realize that none of these ads are
directed to women. I don't know of one woman who
owns an insurance policy, because they're all strong as
bulls. Nothing is going to keep *them* out of the picture.

Insurance statistics prove that women live longer
than men, and there's a reason for this: they're not
married to women. When a man dies, women never
discuss what a good husband or father he was. What
they always ask is, "How did he leave her?" Well, a lot
of them were glad to go.

But even the insurance companies realize that some
men just don't give up this easily, so they have an ad
which always pictures this old gray-haired couple fishing in Florida. And the caption reads: "How I Retired
on Thirty-five Dollars a Week in Sunny Florida."

Has anybody who's read this ad *been* to Florida on
thirty-five dollars a week? You know where this couple
retired? To the Everglades. Their next-door neighbor is

a crocodile. And the reason they're always seen fishing is because they're hungry. They've got to eat, you know.

Now the greatest insurance salesman is your wife. The minute you sign the marriage certificate, directly underneath it is the insurance policy. Of course, she has to have help—*her* brother. Nobody ever buys insurance from a stranger. Everybody's got a relative in the business, and my wife's brother is *it* in our family.

He goes up to Hartford once a month for brainwashing. They check the buttons on his suit, see that his lapels are narrow enough for the job, and give him the party line. Then they turn him loose on his relatives.

I was sitting at home the other afternoon when he showed up. He walked into the living room, gave me a dazzling smile, and stuck out his hand.

"How do you do, sir," he said.

"What 'sir'?" I asked him. "It's me. Your brother-in-law."

But no, he kept right on. They're all taught to sell insurance the same way, you know. They all come up with the same line, "I'm sure that after I conduct my business with you, you're going to sleep better tonight."

"What 'business'?" I inquired. "Will somebody tell me what this is all about?"

"Now, sir," he said, "what type of insurance are you carrying?"

"My GI policy," I told him.

"Is that all?" He looked shocked. "My, my." In the

insurance business they all say "My, my." It's part of the training program.

"What's wrong with a GI policy? It carried me through a war when people were shooting at me."

"Oh," he said, "that was all right when you were younger. Now you have responsibilities. You're a married man with a family. Do you want this charming woman—"

"That's your sister," I told him. "Look, let's just skip all this. Do you just want to give me a nice, quiet policy, without any aggravation?"

"Certainly, sir," he said. "I have taken the liberty of drawing up a list of your needs. I have a few ideas that I think will fill the bill."

That's how I now happen to have a retirement policy, straight life, twenty-payment term, an endowment policy for my two boys, and college insurance. I have health and accident, hospitalization, medical, major medical (which means you've got to have a sick major in the house in order to collect), mortgage cancellation, travel insurance, water damage, general floater and fire-and-theft.

I have automobile insurance that consists of personal property, liability, fifty dollars deductible, collision, and theft.

I've got crop insurance, too. I've got an acre of land that can't even grow grass, but I've got crop insurance. I have a policy that says if an iceberg is sighted between Norfolk, Virginia, and St. Petersburg, Florida, I get fifty dollars.

I have hole-in-one golf insurance. The tradition is that if you get a hole-in-one you have to buy everybody in the locker room champagne. Now the statistics are something like four million to one of my ever getting a hole-in-one, but if I do, the insurance company will pick up the tab for champagne.

I'm going to be paying out so much of my income to take care of the future that I'll be starving to death in the present. It boils down to the fact that I've got to believe in the hereafter because I'm insured for that, too.

Now some of these policies are very easy to get. You give them money and they give you the policy. But the more important policies with higher premiums have to do something to justify the cost, so you have to be put through a test.

The first part of the test is the written application. The insurance company wants to know all about your health. The application form contains questions like, "Did your grandmother ever have a hangnail?" and "List all your relatives who died, and why." One read, "Do you have good eyes?" and the print was so small that just by reading the question you passed the test.

They ask, "Do you Smoke? Drink? Drive a car? Fly?" I put down "No" to everything. I didn't want to upset the insurance company. I'm going to take my policies and lock myself in a closet because I don't want them to take any chances with me.

They always ask, "How old are you?" and I wrote down "Eighty-four" as a gag. When I took the application back, the insurance examiner at the desk looked at the age and said, "You're so lucky because I can just get you in under the old existing rates."

My fire-and-theft policies came through while I was waiting on the life insurance. Jeanette and I went away for a three-day weekend and when we came back, we found the house had been robbed. I love things to be done well, and these thugs really did a job. They must have made eight trips and used a van. With talent like that, you can't get mad.

When I called the insurance company to report the theft, they asked me, "What kind of policy did you say you have?"

"Fire and theft," I told them.

"My, my," said the woman on the other end, "that's too bad. You should have had Fire *or* Theft." According to her, the only way I could collect would be if I was robbed while the house was burning down.

The life insurance policies require you to take a physical examination and finally they called me over. I was a little nervous. I sat in the waiting room with a bunch of other candidates awaiting my turn. Now I don't know if you've ever noticed or not, but doctors have the oldest magazines in existence in their offices. Even the New York Public Library doesn't have the copies they do. While I was right in the middle of reading about the sinking of the *Lusitania,* the guy next to me began jumping up and down and waving his newspaper. "Hey, lookit!" he yelled. "Lindy landed!"

Of course, I haven't much faith in doctors anyway. If I can ever find anybody who practices medicine the way Jean Hersholt did, I'll be happy. I frankly don't see how doctors find time to practice much these days —they're all too busy testing cigarettes and watching liver bile flow.

And, of course, no doctor today will make house calls any more. I know one doctor who won't make any call where he has to climb stairs. He's afraid of his heart.

After the usual two hours of waiting, I was called into the doctor's office. I found out that insurance doctors aren't like the rest of them. They don't even examine you. All you have to do is fill up a bottle. I don't know what they do with all the filled bottles, but if anybody can figure out a use for them, he'll make a fortune. This is the guy I should have been bringing my deposit bottles to.

In and out of several insurance doctors' offices as I was, I learned one thing: if the doctor's doing well, *he* supplies the bottle. In a poor doctor's office, you have to bring your own.

With all my new policies, my wife is very happy. When I leave for work in the morning, she smiles brightly and says, "Have a nice day, darling. Take chances."

You'd think that now my problems would be over—but it never works out that way. Before I got all these new policies I had been paying for insurance with one company for fifteen years. We got along fine. I never had a claim; I paid my premiums on time; I never really gave insurance a thought.

But just about six weeks ago I had an accident, and what happened to me is typical of what I think you can expect when you're insured the way I am.

One night I was visiting in midtown Manhattan, my car was parked by the curb and I came back to find one side of the car smashed in. I took the car to a local garage where I was told the repair bill would amount to $270. Well, I had $50 deductible so I called my insurance company.

Now the first voice you hear when you call up any insurance company belongs to a very important official. The job of the person who answers the phone is to prevent you from getting through to anybody else. If you get past her, she's fired.

Now the first thing she said to me was, "Who sold you the policy?"

"My brother-in-law, Murray Bensen," I told her.

She said, "I'm sorry, but he's no longer with the company."

"Since when?"

"Since the minute you had that accident."

"Well, look," I told her. "My name is Alan King and

I have a claim to make. I've got twenty policies with your company and I've *had* an accident."

"My, my," she said.

"Look," I warned her, "if you start with the 'my, my,' I'm going to come after you."

"Have you registered this accident with the police department?" she asked.

"No," I told her. "They don't carry my policy."

"Well, sir," she said, "you have to fill out an XJ-347 form and mail it in. Don't fix the car until we look at it, and wait for our adjuster."

In a literal translation of the Old Testament, it says that "The Messiah will come, riding a white ass over a bridge of paper." Now, *He'll* be here before the adjuster.

For weeks I rode around with my right hand on the wheel and my left hand holding up the door. Finally, the insurance company sent me a nice young man—typical of the breed—in a nine-button suit, thin lapels, no shoulders. He looked at the car and said,

"That's not too bad."

"I agree with you, sir," I told him. "Now do you want to look at the side of the car that was hit?"

"My, my," he said.

"Now the damages are $270," I told him. "I have a $50 deductible policy with you and I'd just like to have the $220."

"How fast were you going when the accident occurred?" he asked me.

140

"I wasn't going anywhere. The car was parked."

"Was the car being used for business or for pleasure?"

"I was visiting my in-laws," I told him. "You figure it out. Do you want to give me the $220?"

"Well, sir, you don't seem to understand. Our head adjuster will be in next week from Detroit—"

"No, no, no. Look, let's not— No head adjuster from Detroit."

"But, sir—"

"Just give me $220," I told him. "I see your ads on television. A guy had an automobile accident. He was pinned under the car and the adjuster was pushing the money *underneath* the car to him. Now you want to give me the money??? I'll take $220."

"Oh," he said, with a pleased smile, "I remember that one. A very fortunate accident. It was our adjuster who hit him."

"I'll take $200," I told him.

"Sir," he pleaded. "Please listen. As I was saying—"

"I saw a fellow's house burn down on television," I told him. "The adjuster was on the fire truck helping with the water *with* the check. Now you want to give me—"

"Sir," he said, "we do not pay out money indiscriminately. After all, this is your money and we are trying to protect it."

"Don't protect my—just give—I have $50,000 paid

141

in, in your company. In premiums. Now you want to give me— I'll take $180."

"Well, sir," he said, "we have to send the report to the home office in Minneapolis."

"Don't give me with Minneapolis. I see your ads on television, where you've got—there's a map of the United States and there are a lotta dots that are supposed to represent offices, and I live in New York and the New York area's got lots of dots.

"I could understand that in New Mexico there's no dots. If I happened to be an Indian who had an accident in New Mexico, you have to send to Minneapolis, but there's plenty of dots in— Look," I was really getting alarmed, "you want to give me—how much? How much now? I'll take a hundred and a quarter."

He shook his head.

"You want to give me a hammer and a can of paint?" I asked him. "Give me a hammer and a can of paint. I'll do it myself."

"No, sir," he said, "you just don't seem to understand. We *have* to send the report to Detroit."

"Listen, do I have personal liability with your company?"

"Yes," he said, "I guess you do."

"Are *you* insured?"

"Why?"

"Because I'm going to beat your brains out—right now."

"You're not covered," he said, positively. "But if you're interested, I could show you—"

You see, they're all alike. What I really want to make you understand about this story is that if you're driving in the New York area and you happen to see my car, I wish you wouldn't wave to me because I won't be able to wave back. I'm still holding up the goddamned door.

[12] A Night on the Town, Did You Say???

WHENEVER I LOOK BACK over my fifteen years of marriage, I realize that, despite how I may sometimes sound, I have little to criticize. I'm a happily married man. Jeanette is an ideal wife and a good mother. She makes my home the kind of place I long to get back to after a hard day's work in the city. That's why I can never understand why it is that the one night a man wants to stay home and relax is *always* the night that his wife wants to go out.

The most frequent complaint a man hears from his wife is: "You never take me out! I'm sick and tired of being cooped up in this house. I want a night on the town."

Their motto is: Put a little fun in your life. Try Spending!

Women don't seem to realize how much it costs just to go out for an evening. I'm not talking about such elegant and well-known places as El Morocco or Twenty One. I'm talking about a plain, simple evening out.

Let's suppose that, like most husbands, you say to your wife, "All right. Why not? You deserve a little fun. Get dressed, we're going out tonight."

Now I guarantee that the first thing out of her mouth will be, "I can't go out looking like this."

Since it's a very difficult thing to tell her that she's got no time for plastic surgery, you let her have her way—she goes to the beauty parlor. This obsession with the hairdresser is something I can never understand. Women—who crossed the plains in covered wagons, fought off the Indians, won the right to vote, and today repair the plumbing with a hairpin—are totally incapable of doing their own hair at home.

I see all these television commercials with all the shampoos and the do-it-yourself home permanents, but ask your wife why *she* doesn't subscribe to this, and you're liable to hear what I hear at my house. "Home permanents," she tells me, "I wear at home."

No matter how simple an evening you're planning,

there isn't a woman who can get out of the beauty parlor for under five dollars, and my wife makes it closer to twenty. She gets:

Shampoo:	$1.50
Finger Wave:	$3.00
Rinse:	$2.00
Manicure:	$2.50
Pedicure:	$3.00
Eyebrow Arch	$1.50
Beauty Parlor:	$13.50
Tips:	3.00
Total:	$16.50

She spends all this money and makes all these beauty preparations just to sit in a dark movie.

Now she's all fixed up—but you can't go yet. The next problem is a baby sitter. Most women don't have sleep-in help, so they have to plan ahead and get somebody in. You just can't leave the kids home alone, your relatives are all booked up, so you telephone around for a sitter.

Telephone call: $0.10

That's if you happen to be lucky the first time. Getting a baby sitter is not as easy as you think. They're

147

all organized. You don't hire a baby sitter today, you put in a sealed bid, and then you have to negotiate.

"If you're not doing anything tonight, dear, would you like to sit for us?" you ask her.

She comes right back with, "What do you have to offer?"

"Well," you say, "I have a handsome eight-room house, air conditioning, wall-to-wall carpets, television, full refrigerator, unlimited phone calls, and if you take a liking to one of my kids, you can have one."

"Do you have stereophonic binaural living sound?"

"No-o-o," you say, "but I tell you what. You come on over and I'll sing for you. Now do you want to sit for me tonight?"

"We get a dollar and a half an hour, with a five-hour minimum," she says.

You can get a registered nurse for a dollar twenty-five an hour. It would be cheaper if your kids were sick. So now you've got:

```
Baby Sitter:    $7.50
```

Finally, you're ready to leave. You say goodbye to the kids and warn them to be nice to the sitter so she'll come again sometime. Your wife, for once, is ready when you are, and the two of you go out to the car. Now you don't just put the clutch into neutral and coast your way into New York. You have to buy gas.

Gas: $3.00

That's for Brand X. With what the evening's going to cost, you can't afford the more expensive fuel.

Now you're on your way—or are you? Strange as it may seem in other parts of the country, the State of New York does not just let you zoom into Manhattan without a charge. There are *tolls*. You've heard the expression "Highway Robbery"? That's where they got it. Wherever you go, there's a dirty hand with a handball glove. The minimum toll charge from the suburbs to the city is thirty-five cents. But you're unfortunately not going to spend the rest of your life in the city. You have to come back:

Tolls: $0.70

So far you've spent $27.80 and you haven't done anything yet. Now the *real* expenses begin.

Have you ever tried to park a car in the city? All the great scientific brains in the nation are trying to send rockets into space, trying to fire missiles thousands of miles into the air, or trying to fly a plane five thousand miles an hour. Just let one of them try to figure out fifteen lousy feet of space for me to park a car. You drive for blocks—up one street and down another—

149

and if there *is* a space available, there's always a little sign that reads:

**PARKING
REGULATIONS**

**NO PARKING ON
ALTERNATE
PALM SUNDAYS
EXCEPT ON WEST
BOUND STREETS
6 TO 7 A.M.
12 TO 2 P.M.
EXCEPT IN
FEBRUARY**

All of this is printed on a metal board a little larger than an electric wall plate and it's like taking an eye test. While you're reading the sign, a miserable little foreign car sneaks into the space.

Because of incredible regulations like these we're all at the mercy of something called "the parking lot." There's no problem in finding a parking lot in New York these days. They're all easily identified by the sign in front which reads, "Sorry, Full Up." For the small fee of one dollar—better known as "payola"—they usually just happen to have space for one more car.

Payola: $1.00

This transaction, of course, takes place *before* you read the rate sign. I don't know if you've ever parked a car in a New York garage, but Wernher von Braun couldn't figure out the rates. On a big board, affixed near the entrance to the parking lot or garage, you'll see something like this:

PARKING RATES / **CUSTOMER PARKING**

Day Rate:

Monday-Friday—6 a.m.-6 p.m.

.75	first ½ hour or part
$1.00	first hour or part
$1.50	two hours or part
$1.50	to 6 p.m.
.50	each additional hour or part
$2.75	Maximum 12 hours
$4.50	Maximum 24 hours

Night Rate:

Monday-Friday—6 p.m.-6 a.m. or part: $2.75
Maximum: $4.50   24 hours

Saturday—6 p.m.-6 a.m. or part: $2.50
Maximum: $4.50   24 hours

Sunday—6 p.m.-6 a.m. or part: $2.75
Maximum: $4.50   24 hours

CAPACITY: 250 cars   **LICENSE:** #429726

151

All you want to do is park the car for a couple of hours, but your minimum cost will be $2.75 (except Saturdays), plus something for the delinquent who destroys your car. If you ever want to get even with a parking attendant, wait until he brings up your car and then say, "What's that scratch doing on the fender?"

Without even looking, he'll snap back, "It was on the car when you came in."

Thumb your nose and repeat after me, "There is no scratch on the car."

You'll still have to tip him, of course, but it makes you feel better.

Parking: $3.00

After the preparations at the beauty parlor, the baby sitter, the gasoline, the tolls, and the parking lot, you've almost forgotten what you came to the city for—but your wife will remind you.

You're having a plain evening out, remember? This means that you head for a Broadway movie that *won't* get to the suburbs for another two years. On the surface it seems like a pretty sound idea, but have you noticed the movie prices lately? When I was a kid the local cinema was two for a nickel. We used to stand out front and yell, "I got two. Who's got three?" In the theater of my youth, they gave you two pictures, an ice cream bar, and a comic book—and you spent a nice day.

Things have changed considerably since that time.

Now, any first-run movie house charges a dollar eighty minimum for a seat. That's until you finally reach the box office. Then the prices change to two twenty.

"Two, please," you tell the cashier.

"I'm sorry," she says, "but all we have left is the Smoking Section. That's two eighty."

So you don't smoke. For two eighty, you'd better develop the habit. Or better yet, you can just sit up there and cough. You can make believe.

Movie Tickets: $5.60

I suppose you've noticed that there are no short pictures any more. Everything's a Biblical spectacular, running time: four hours; intermissions: two. It's becoming more and more difficult these days to be a nonbeliever.

Because of the length of the film, you'll starve to death without food, so you buy some candy inside the theater. Now there are no nickel candy bars any more. To be in keeping with the price of the tickets and the grandeur of the wide screen, candy now comes giftwrapped like an anniversary present. So now you have:

Candy: $0.50

During the movie you have an excellent opportunity to figure out that—with time out for intermissions, and the drive into the city and back—you'll be paying overtime to the baby sitter. If the movie is terrible anyway,

153

you might as well occupy your mind with all the cloudy thoughts of the money that's going uselessly down the drain.

Eventually, of course, even the spectacular will come to a churning halt and, as you come out of the movie, your wife—who started the whole thing in the beginning—will undoubtedly say, "We just can't come out of the picture and go straight home. Let's have some Chinese food."

At home, on her money, she's on a diet; with you, she has to have Chinese food. This may not sound too expensive because in any Chinese restaurant the cheapest dish is bound to be fried rice. Around Broadway, however, written in Cantonese, Mandarin, and plain American, the price reads: one dollar fifty a portion. In China for one dollar fifty you could buy the whole rice paddy. I think probably the proprietors of these restaurants are trying to get even for Formosa.

When your check arrives, it adds up to three dollars plus entertainment tax. And if you are so foolish as to inquire what the entertainment tax is for, you'll probably learn that the waiter was humming "Love Is a Many-Splendored Thing."

Supper	$3.00
Tip:	$1.00
Total:	$4.00

You add it all up if you want to. But I can save you the time. Your total is $41.90—for a plain, simple evening out. Do you men realize what this means? If you didn't go out for one year, you could send your child to college.

Men, do me a favor.

The next time you come home and your wife says to you, "You never take me out," look her straight in the eye and say, "Do you mean to stand there and tell me that just for an evening's frivolity, you'd deprive our son of a college education?"

[13] GO UPSTAIRS
And Give Those
Kids a Beating

IF THERE'S ONE TENET that all women share in common, it's this: a woman's work is never done.

Women lead a hard life. They work from sunrise until late in the evening, and they have a thousand different worries each day in raising the children and taking care of the house. By contrast, a man is carefree. He has no responsibilities, no problems, no worries, they'll tell you. That's *their* story.

Now how much time do women actually spend with their children? The kids are always out of the house. They go to private school, public school, nursery school, dancing school, Sunday school, Boy Scouts, Girl Scouts —and other children's parties. They're always away from home.

A school bus picks them up early in the morning and brings them home late at night. If you give the driver a few dollars extra, he'll leave the kid at another house for a few days. I've got a new boy running around my house now and I don't know who the hell he is. He eats with chopsticks. He's a nice boy, but I don't know him.

If nobody claims him before school is out, he goes to summer camp with my two sons. We don't fool around at our house. Anybody who's there when school is out goes to summer camp. It's a rule.

My wife can't wait for summer to come. She starts sewing the labels on the boys' summer clothes in December. She says the kids make her nervous. Now my mother had eight children and she was never nervous. We kids were nervous, but my mother—never. And none of us ever got to go to summer camp.

In my neighborhood only the sick and undernourished children could go. The politicians would come along and select the winners off the streets. They'd step down from the curb and tap the lucky ones on the shoulder, "You, you, you—you're going to camp." When they came to me, they'd say, "You're getting a job."

One fellow in our neighborhood went to summer camp five years in a row. He was a forty-three-year-old jockey, but he got picked every time.

Today the politicians are too busy sending men to the moon; they don't have time for summer camp any more, so it's up to the parents. And the cost of these summer camps today is almost as expensive as *going* to the moon.

Of course, on the day my kids leave for summer camp, my wife suddenly acts as though she hasn't been trying to get rid of them all year. We take them to the railroad station and she starts carrying on. "They're going away," she sobs, "I don't think I can stand it. It's going to be so lonely around the house."

Then my boys yell, "We're not going!"

"Get on the train," she screams, "or I'll have a breakdown."

She runs to the conductor. "Seal up the car, rev up the engines. Get them out of here. I'm so nervous!"

"What are you nervous about?" I often ask her.

"What do you know about what goes on here?" she'll counter. "I have to look after the children, cook the food, and run this big house."

Well, this would sound great coming from almost any other woman in the United States, but not my wife. We've got three in help.

We've got one maid who sleeps in for fifty dollars a week. That's all she does. She sleeps in. Then we've got a maid who comes in for the heavy work on Friday.

Her job is to wake the other one up. Sometimes we have to use a pulmotor.

We also have a nurse. When my youngest son, Andy, was born, my wife said she'd like a nurse for the baby until she could get back on her feet. That was eight years ago. Our nurse is a lovely woman, she resembles John Wayne. She's about six foot three inches tall, Swedish, and she eats as though she's going to the electric chair. Every afternoon she takes a nap. I wish my children slept as well as the nurse. If one of them has to go to the bathroom in the middle of the night, my wife will say, "Sssh, you'll wake up the nurse."

Now with all the help we have in the house, my wife—a really conscientious mother—will never take a holiday unless *my* mother is there to supervise everything. I have six sisters-in-law who feel the same way, which makes my mother a very busy woman.

My brothers' wives are always calling her up. "Hello, Mom, where've you been? The children miss you." Then they'll say, "Why don't you and Dad come over for a few days. No, it won't be crowded. You can use our room. We're leaving in the morning for three weeks."

My mother really enjoys this because all she lives for are her grandchildren. When you call her up, she doesn't wait to find out who you are. She says, "I can't come today. Tom has me today, then Eddie gets me for a week, and then Anita has me from the twentieth on, indefinitely."

My mother is booked until 1966. She hasn't seen my

father in five and a half years and he's happy about the whole thing. For the first time in his life, *he's* not nervous.

Because of all the progressive "how to raise your children" books, and the permissiveness we parents display, and the coddling of grandparents, children today are spoiled completely. They're used to having everything they want because they're never denied anything. This makes them hard to manage because they've never been taught to obey.

A few weeks ago I came home after a full day of television rehearsals. I was exhausted and I couldn't wait to get in the house and leave the problems of the day behind me. If I'd known what I was in for, I would have kept on driving. Jeanette was having trouble with the boys.

I parked the car in the driveway and, as I was getting out, I could hear my wife inside the house. "I've let you get away with it all day," she yelled, "and now you're going to get it. You've tried my patience for the last time. Now *he's* here." She made it sound as though King Kong had arrived. The villain was about to enter the scene.

I walked into the house not knowing what to expect. Jeanette was the only person in sight, and for a moment I wondered if she had been talking to herself. The minute she spotted me, she said, "You're home!"

"How'd you figure it out? What'd you do, recognize the car?"

"Don't make jokes with me, Alan," she said, wearily. "You don't know what I've been through. You should have been here this afternoon. It was like the Civil War all over again—brother against brother." She sank down into a chair. "I just don't know what to do any more. I want you to go upstairs and give those kids a beating."

"I just walked in," I told her. "Let me take my coat off . . . I hit better." She just sat there, waiting. "Tell me," I said, "what did they do?"

"What did they do?" she sighed. "What didn't they do?"

"What is this, a riddle? Give me a little hint so I can hate them."

She said, "I can't take it from those boys any more. They're driving me to an early grave."

"Don't move," I told her, "let me do it. I'll get the car."

"You're just like your sons," she said, "they take after you."

Now that's fairly typical in an argument of this kind, you know. When they're bad, they're mine.

"Jeanette," I pleaded. "Just compose yourself and tell me—what did they do?"

She burst into tears. "They beat each other up," she sobbed. "They had a fight."

"Then what's the sense of my beating them up, too? They've already taken care of each other."

Well, this nonsense continued for another twenty

minutes. Jeanette insisted the boys had to be punished; I figured they'd punished each other. The entire discussion got completely out of control and finally, when she said for about the tenth time, "Go upstairs and give those kids a beating," I had worked myself up into the proper rage and I started up the stairs.

Now I had my foot on the third step from the bottom when she yelled loud enough to be heard two houses away, *"Don't hit them any more."* That, of course, was the only part of the argument the neighbors heard. I can just picture it—I'm walking through the neighborhood, conscious of unseen eyes watching my progress down the street. "There he goes—the child-beater." It will be no use for me to protest, as I did to Jeanette, that I hadn't even seen the kids yet. My reputation is firmly established by now.

Of course, in this day and age, children are not punished by spanking. We give them severe penalties like, "I'm cutting your allowance down to five dollars a week," or "All right, you'll get no supper. Go to your room."

Let's investigate this last tough punishment, which my wife invokes frequently. In my boys' room there are: an electric train set, a television set, eleven boxes of cookies, seventeen candy bars, and one hundred assorted comic books.

The comic books—with their emphasis on horror, murder, mayhem, and science fiction—really help us shape these little monsters we're raising.

One night, playing the part of a good father, I sat down with my older son, Bobby, for a man-to-man talk. During the course of it, he volunteered to tell me a story he'd heard in Sunday school. "It's really interesting, Dad," he said. "I think you'll enjoy it."

"Sure, Bob," I agreed, "let's hear it."

"Well," he began, "once there was a planet called Tartarus which was orbiting too close to the sun, and all the people on it were doomed, because pretty soon it was going to crash into the sun and burn up.

"Now there was a scientist and his wife who wanted to save their son and so they put him in the nose cone of a rocket and got ready to blast him off to earth.

"The baby landed in Egypt in the Nile River. There was a very rich girl, a Pharaoh's daughter, who was skin diving, and she came upon this nose cone. She opened it up and there was the baby, so she decided to take him home and raise him as her own, and she named him Moses.

"Moses was raised as a prince, but the Pharaoh— this girl's old man—was a miserable coot and he had a lot of people around as slaves. As Moses was growing up he got to talking to these people and he found out they all came from the same planet he came from, and he didn't like to see them as slaves.

"So one day he walked into the Pharaoh's private office, stuck a gun in the old guy's back, and said, 'All right. This is it! Let my people go. I'm not askin' ya, I'm tellin' ya.'

164

"Now they started to move out—and I mean, they moved! They got to a big ocean, and it looked like they were stopped. But Moses was a smart cookie, and he'd thought this all out before. He had the engineers build a pontoon bridge, and they all crossed over. But here came the bad guys after them. Again, Moses was smart. He had the bridge detonated. It blew up and killed all the bad guys, and Moses and the rest of his people were saved."

There was, understandably, I think, a moment of silence when he had finished. Then I found my voice: "This is what they told you in Sunday school?" I asked him.

"Yeh."

"Come on, Bobby," I said. "Is this *really* what they told you in Sunday school?"

"Well, not exactly, Dad," he confessed. "But if I told you what they told us, you'd never believe it."

[14] Hubert Wellington, III

I'M NOT TOO CRAZY ABOUT DOGS.

Now before you slam this book down and rush out to call the ASPCA, let me explain.

You see, I'm a little leery of *some* animal lovers. You've seen the type—they dye their dogs pink, deck them out in rhinestones, and give them names like Suzy or Pierre. I may be wrong, but it's always seemed to me that anybody who carries on that way about an animal doesn't have too much faith and trust in people.

These kinds of pet lovers have been hurt by someone someplace along the way, and so they shower all their love on the animal.

A dog *owner*—like me—is different. We're not "dedicated" to the animal. We don't dislike him, but we don't get carried away by him either.

I didn't have a dog when I was a child. My parents said they had enough mouths to feed. I grew up without knowing the love and affection of a dog and, to tell you the truth, I never really missed it.

So it was with great misgivings that I heard a new sound in our house one day. Somebody said, "I wish we had a dog."

Here we were—in a nice house, in a good neighborhood, with friends around us. What more could we want? Who needs a dog?

But one day I heard it again, "I wish we had a dog."

Why? I wondered. What's so great about a dog? You have to feed him, walk him, take care of him. Dogs can be a lot of trouble. Of course, all the time, I knew I was really arguing with myself. Nobody else would think of these things.

Even Jeanette was for a dog. In her case, I could understand it. She lived in Suburbia, she had a tweed suit with leather patches over the elbows, and a pair of sensible British walking shoes. All she needed to complete the outfit was a dog on the end of a leash. It was like a set, with one piece missing.

I thought about the dog for several weeks and then

one morning I came down to breakfast and announced,
"We're buying a dog." The most surprised person at
the breakfast table was me, and by then it was too late.
Command Decision had been made! To the tune of a
fantastic family ovation, I bowed to the inevitable.
Little did I know what lay ahead.

You don't just go out and buy a dog, you know—
even if you don't go through what *I* did to get one.
And, after you get the dog, what then? You've got to
name him, feed him, house him, and get along with
him. It's like taking in a roomer.

The only knowledge I had of dogs came from pet
shops. I used to watch those cute little puppies on the
cut paper in the pet-shop windows, and I found out
that those puppies were like shills. They were the come-
on for the ugly dogs in the back, because you could
never buy one of the dogs in the window. They weren't
for sale.

Jeanette didn't want a pet-shop dog anyway. Her
idea was for me to drive up to Connecticut and buy
a pedigreed dog from a kennel. After talking me into
the trip, she was too smart to go along herself. "Surprise me," she said. Those were her last words before
we left.

Now this is the first thing to avoid when you're buying a dog: Never let yourself get trapped into making
a long trip to a kennel. It can have most unexpected
results.

Those of you with children of your own can imagine

the kind of trip I had. We weren't even out of the driveway before one of the boys said, "Daddy, how soon before we get there?" When they weren't inquiring about our arrival, they were jumping up and down on the back seat, yelling, "We're getting a dog! We're getting a dog!"

It was a miserable trip—with the traffic, the chanting, and the questions. I also discovered that I should have had a built-in bathroom put in the car. We made so many stops I began to get worried. Where is it all coming from? I wondered.

After an hour and a half's driving—not counting the stops—I saw the name of the kennel, painted on a white Colonial sign board, and we turned off the main road and drove up a long, winding tree-shaded drive to an eighteenth-century farmhouse set in immaculate lawns, with rows of wire pens for the dogs stretching away toward the back.

A man came out to greet us. Now I don't know what your conception of a kennel master is—but this one wore riding breeches. I began right away to worry about the size of the dogs he'd show us. Besides the breeches, he had thick black hair and a wispy little moustache.

"EE-yesss?" he said, as he drew near. "What can I do for *you?*"

He talked just like the Great Gildersleeve, and with my built-in resentment over the whole trip, I was all prepared to dislike him.

"I'd like to see a dog," I told him.

"A dawg?" he drawled, rather doubtfully, a slight frown forming around his moustache.

"Yes," I said.

"You want a dawg?" he asked again.

I was beginning to get a little sore. "What the hell else you got here?" I asked him.

"Well, sir," he began, in an aggrieved voice, "I'm *trying* to discover what type of dog you would like."

"A dog," I told him. "A plain dog. With ears. With a tail. With barking." I didn't seem to be getting through. "You know," I said, trying to leave it up to his imagination, "a dog."

"But, dear sir," he intoned, "we have different *breeds*. We have cockers, boxers, terriers."

"That sounds good. Let me see one of those."

He looked at me for a moment. "Won't you sit down?" he asked.

"No," I told him. "I don't want to try him on. Just let me see some dogs."

He invited me back toward the wire pens. "Look around," he said, airily waving his hand, "perhaps you'll see something that impresses you."

And I did. I saw this long, pointed face with a pink tongue and floppy hair. It was the owner's wife. If you could ever have thrown a leash on her, you'd make a fortune.

I was still looking around when my feet suddenly left the ground and my head came down hard in their place. A large cat was streaking away in front of me and, hard after it, the dog that had apparently caused my downfall. He was short, but compact. Going as fast as he was, it was difficult to get much idea of his shape, but he did carry an outsized feather duster which, for him, masqueraded as a tail. The rest of his features were not clearly discernible, covered as he was with woolly, battleship-gray-colored hair.

My two boys were jumping up and down excitedly, the dog was barking, the cat was yowling, and the kennel master was wringing his hands.

"Oh, no," he cried. "Will you *look* at that filthy animal?"

I could hardly hear him because the boys were yelling, "We want that dog! We want that Dog! We want that DOG!"

"*That* dog?" I could hardly believe my ears.

The kennel master intervened. "I wouldn't think of it, Mr. King," he said. "That's not our dog. He's a stray who keeps coming around here."

The kids persisted.

"Look," I told the kennel master. "I don't know much about dogs but the kids seem to like him. I'll take him off your hands."

"Well," he said, "I couldn't just *give* him to you."

"Why not?"

"You must realize that after all—this is a *kennel*. We *sell* dogs."

"I thought you said he was a stray."

"Ah, yes," he sighed. "It's true—but a very important stray, nonetheless. Look how much exercise he gives our cats."

We looked at each other for a minute. "All right," I said, "how much?"

"Would five dollars seem unreasonable?"

"Yes."

"It's a deal." He beamed happily. "I'll just get a rope and try to catch him."

We drove home that night in peaceful coexistence. Nobody jumped up and down in the car, or asked questions, or suggested we stop at the next gas station. The dog sat in the middle of the back seat as though he'd always belonged, and on either side were my kids, each with an arm flung possessively around his new pal. I was tired but satisfied, because my kids were happy. What did it matter that I'd driven all the way to Connecticut to a fine pedigreed kennel to buy a dog I could have picked up in the streets?

My only worry was how Jeanette would take it. She hadn't envisioned an ordinary dog. Like most people, she wanted a dog she could be proud of, one whose pedigree she could faithfully recite.

Right there—on the way home—I decided not to disappoint her. So, before I go any further, I want your cooperation. If you ever meet my wife, don't let on. You see, she doesn't know there's no such thing as a Mongolian Problapup. She thinks it's a very rare breed.

173

Well, now I have become a dog owner. I've satisfied my kids, made my wife very happy. I figured now all I had to do was relax and watch the kids and the dog romp around. Well, I was wrong. There's more to it than that. You've got to name the dog, you know. A name is very important.

I just don't understand all this craziness in naming a dog. The dogs I used to read about were called Rex or Buck or Fido. Today people border on the ridiculous in naming a dog. They give them names like Shepard's Rock of Crosstown, and Robin of Roselyn Heights. The champion dog at the Westminster Dog Show a few years ago was named Baxter Benjamin VII. The woman who owned him was married to a man named Abe and had two kids named Izzie and Melvin, but the dog was called Baxter Benjamin VII.

At our house, we held a family conference to pick the name of the dog. When the boys were born, my wife named each one in three minutes flat. The dog's name took five and a half hours to select.

I was the one who finally named him, after seeing that every sensible name had been turned down. Each time I suggested a good dog-type name, my wife exercised her right of veto. Finally, in an effort to show how ridiculous I thought it all was, I said, "Let's name him Hubert Wellington III," and she thought it was an inspiration. Even the boys didn't object. They don't have to call him anyway—he's always right by their side.

174

So here we are—Alan, Jeanette, Bobby, and Andy—and Hubert Wellington III. One thing I know—with a name like that and with engraving costs going up, he's going to have to send out his *own* Christmas cards.

Right after we named him, Jeanette started to plan his diet and care. You don't just feed a dog table scraps any more, you know. You have to go at this the right way, particularly if you happen to have a fine pedigreed dog like ours.

You must also be careful to raise your animals properly. Jeanette went out and bought a book on animal care and she started to raise Hubert just the way she raised the kids. As a matter of fact, I think she bought the same book. She got Dr. Spock for Hubert.

She takes him to get his nails clipped, his tail brushed, and his hair cut. She carries on as though he were a human being. One day when she couldn't get Hubert an appointment at *his* barber shop, she wanted me to take him to mine. I could just see somebody walking in and the barber saying, "You'll have to wait. The dog is next."

She feeds him vitamin A, thiamin, B-1 complex, riboflavin, and niacin. I don't understand why she's carrying on with this Madame Curie menu. The dog was living out of garbage pails and off cats when I first saw him. I think she'll kill him with this kind of diet, but every time I say anything, she tells me, "Alan, you just do not understand about dogs."

She watches all the TV commercials that advertise

175

dog food and these are some of the funniest ads in the world.

You know the one where the announcer says, "What do you think of this food?" and the dog says, "Rrufff." Now what is he *really* saying when he barks? The director probably stepped on his foot or slapped him just before he went on camera and that's why he barked. But the announcer always tells you, "Three out of four dogs had that same thing to say about Dog-go."

Then they show you two dogs that look exactly alike. The announcer says, "One dog is forty-two years old, and the other dog is six years old, but the forty-two-year-old has been raised on Dog-go. Which one is the great-grandfather?" I thought my son Andy had the best answer to that. He said, "The older one."

To clinch the sale, they have two dog bowls—one filled with "Brand X" and the other, with the sponsor's food. Nearby is a dog on a leash and the announcer says, "Now when I release the leash, watch and see which bowl the dog goes to."

Of course the dog goes to their product—but they don't tell you what's in that other bowl. I think that they probably have some chopped-up gym socks or a mangled rubber inner tube which, under any conditions, the dog would never go to. The ideal dog food, it seems to me, would be one that tastes like a mailman. I think that would be a big seller.

Our dog doesn't really care what the food tastes like. He'll eat anything. He's not finicky about food. The only thing he's really particular about is his doghouse. Jeanette called in a carpenter to build Hubert a roomy house of his own. When it was finally complete, it had windows, a big opening in front for Hubert to go in and out, and a foam rubber carpet wall to wall.

Hubert has developed a real affection for that doghouse. He doesn't sleep in it, of course, but he collects things and deposits them there, like in a bank. Most of his loot he pilfers from the neighbors' clotheslines. He's got enough old clothes to open up his own thrift shop.

Of course, you know by now how this story ends. Hubert is a permanent fixture around our place, and he's supplanted me in my kids' lives. They don't need me any more. When they get up to go to the bathroom in the middle of the night, it's Hubert they call to go with them. And bedtime stories are no longer required. They curl up with Hubert and go right to sleep.

Even Jeanette worries more about Hubert than she does about me. One night last winter she woke me up at three in the morning. "Alan, I forgot to remind you before. You'll have to get up and take out the dog." It was 20 above zero and the dog was under the radiator. He didn't want to go out any more than I did. As I was leaving, she called out, "Make sure he's dressed warmly." Now the dog's got his own fur coat; *I'm* the one she should be worrying about. I could have been in my jockey shorts, for all she knew, but it was the dog that was on her mind.

I frankly admit it, I'm a little jealous of Hubert. He's stolen away some of the affection that should, by rights, be mine.

Now I know that every husband and father feels the same way at one time or another, but my family is carrying this whole thing too far. Hubert's even affecting our rare nights out.

Last week we all went to a movie and in the middle of the picture, Jeanette said to me, "Alan, you forgot to take the dog out."

"Don't get so worried," I told her, "he probably saw the picture."

"Oh, Alan," she said, "I think you're jealous. He's just a little dog."

Little dog? Yes, I guess so. But you know that old saying, "Every dog has his day." Well, I'm going to buy a brand-new puppy for this family. Oh, I know what you're thinking. Sure, it'll be a lot of trouble, having two dogs in the house. But let's just see how Hubert likes taking a back seat for a change.

[15] The Angry Man

OVER THE PAST FEW YEARS I've heard a great deal of talk about the angry men. We've had the first angry man, the angry young men, and the last angry man. There doesn't seem to be anybody left who isn't mad about something.

Now I never worried too much about this until— a couple of years ago—somebody called me an angry man, and that burned me up! There is a great deal of difference between the angry men and me. These other fellows are angry about the Big Picture—the fate of the arts, the Berlin question, and the thermonuclear bomb.

Frankly, I envy these men. I wish I had the time to vent my spleen on remote and impersonal problems. As a matter of fact, I've tried a couple of times, but something always seems to get in the way—like that exorbitant repair bill from my garage, and the last six shirts I bought that shrank after one washing. Don't think I wouldn't *like* to debate the disarmament question. It's just that I don't have the energy. After arguing about a fifty-cent haircut that costs me two dollars, I'm limp for the rest of the day.

My feeling is that the everyday problems have to be solved *first*. That's why I resent being classed with the angry men. If they don't solve the little problems, how can they expect to come up with the answers to the big ones? As a matter of fact, trying to ignore the problems close to home is half of what's wrong with the world today.

A man who's had a fight with his wife at eight A.M. *can't* be reasonable at a conference table at eleven; a communist with a shrunken shirt is naturally going to seem red-faced and belligerent about Berlin; and a writer whose wife is a demon housekeeper *will* worry about the fate of the Arts if he can't find the penciled notes he carefully left on a pleasantly littered desk yesterday.

Now I think these men have a right to be angry. Their trouble is they're all angry at the wrong things. My kind of anger is more direct and to the point. In some circles, I'm known as a hollerer. I yell a great deal, and people like my wife often say, "What are you always hollering about?"

Well, I feel that hollering is good for you. If more people would yell instead of keeping it all inside, there wouldn't be so many illnesses. Let all the anger come out. What you're actually doing is shouting for your life. If you were in the middle of an ocean and you found yourself drowning, what would you do? You'd holler, *"Help!"* You wouldn't say, "How do you like that? I'm drowning."

You have to apply this same reasoning to everyday living. When you find yourself being pulled under, when something or someone annoys you—speak up! Declare yourself! If you don't somebody will always be taking advantage of you. The world is made up of little dictators trying to boss you around.

For instance, did you ever walk into an empty elevator on a Saturday or Sunday when you had some work to finish in your office? There's nobody there but the elevator operator. As you step in, he says, "Please step to the rear of the car and face the front."

Why should he make this ridiculous statement? What is it with him? The car isn't going to go up if you stand sideways? And if you attempt to argue it with him, he cuts you off with "No talking to the elevator operator, please." Obviously you have to stand your ground. Dare him to start the elevator while you're standing sideways. Make him *prove* to you the damn thing won't go up.

181

Signs are another annoyance on *my* angry man level. Everywhere you go today, there's a sign giving you orders. Right under the traffic light, it says, "WALK" or "DON'T WALK." Maybe *once* I'd like to skip across the street. There's a sign that reads, "THIS IS YOUR CITY. KEEP IT CLEAN." If it's my city, maybe I like to keep it dirty.

Now if we aren't being *ordered* to do something, we're being intimidated in other ways. Last week I went into a barbershop for a shave. Some of these barbershops have watch repairmen who work in a corner or in the window of the shop. The place I went into had a setup like this. Now I never feel that these small businessmen make out too well, so I try to help out, to be a nice fellow. It never pays.

The crystal on my watch was cracked and, as I was going in for a shave anyway, I figured I'd get a new crystal put in while I was in the barber's chair. The watch was running. I just wanted to give the repairman a little business.

I handed him the watch and before I could say anything, he had whipped out a jeweler's loupe, stuck it in his eye, and had begun to examine the watch as though he were Louis Pasteur inspecting an army of bacteria.

"My, my," he said. "Oh, boy!"

"Excuse me," I interrupted, "but what's with the 'my, my' and the 'oh, boy'? You never saw a cracked crystal before?"

182

"Cracked crystal?" he sneered. "You should be that lucky."

"What is it? The radium dial is busted and the whole area is contaminated?"

"You can make jokes," he said. "You know what trouble you got? Have you looked at the mainspring?"

"No-o-o, not lately," I told him. "When I look at the watch, I look at the numbers. What mainspring?"

"You have a bent mainspring, a cracked winding stem *and*, on top of that, the watch is filthy."

"Now watch your language," I warned him. "This is a bad rap. I can just see my reviews tomorrow. 'Alan King had a funny act but his watch was dirty.' Stop giving me a diagnosis. Just put in a new crystal, will you please? The watch is running."

"It won't last a day," he told me.

"Then I'll use a sundial," I yelled. "Just put in the damn crystal."

He shrugged and gave me a dirty look. "Sure, mister," he said, "it's your watch."

"I was beginning to worry."

I went over and settled down in the barber's chair and this same nut came over with the jeweler's loupe still in his eye and started to shave me.

"Wait a minute," I said, "I thought you were a jeweler."

"No," he said, "I'm a barber but I smoke Viceroys and I think for myself and I still say that watch won't last a day."

Well, this sort of experience is frustrating enough. Even worse are the real "pros," the specialists in the world.

One day I had a toothache, a real nerve-tingling, head-jarring toothache. I met a friend of mine, Sam Miller, on the street and told him my troubles.

"Look, Alan," he said, "you shouldn't let a thing like that go. At 1650 Broadway, there's one of the greatest dentists in the world, Dr. Schoenfeld. You go up to him and get that tooth looked after. Tell him I sent you. He'll take care of you right away."

Dr. Schoenfeld's office was on the fifteenth floor. I took the elevator up, walked in and gave my name and that of my friend to his nurse. In just a couple of minutes he called me in.

After the usual "How long have you known Sam?" amenities, I got into the chair and he examined the tooth.

"Well, Mr. King," he said, after a few minutes, "I can see why you're having all that pain. Unfortunately the tooth is beyond saving. It's got to come out. I don't do extractions," said the good doctor, "but there's an excellent dentist on the twelfth floor, Dr. Metcalf. He specializes in extractions. Go down and see him and tell him I sent you."

On the twelfth floor after a fifteen-minute wait, I got in to see Dr. Metcalf. We started with my friend Sam, progressed to Dr. Schoenfeld and my problem. Metcalf was the right man, all right. As he started to extract the tooth, it slipped and I swallowed it.

"My, my," he said. "Haven't had that happen in about fifteen years. Rather exciting for you, I'll bet. Well," he beamed, "don't get panicky. On the tenth floor we've got a fine x-ray man. Let's get a picture right away and find out just where the tooth is. He's in 1026—Dr. Egan."

In 1026 Egan fiddled around getting me positioned just right, shot a couple of pictures and I waited while he got the results. He came out beaming and waving his x ray.

"Perfect picture," he crowed. "Clear as a bell. Your tooth is embedded in the upper colon. Very interesting. Bit unusual, but interesting."

"Thanks," I mumbled weakly.

"Oh, say now," he said, grabbing me by the arm. "Don't take it like that. On the eighth floor there's a wonderful internist, Dr. Wright. Really wonderful. Take this print with you so he can see it. And don't worry about a thing."

I waited a few minutes on the tenth floor for an elevator and then decided to walk down the two flights. I must have jarred the tooth because when I got to the eighth floor, the internist gave me the good news that the tooth was now in my lower colon.

"Now what?" I asked him.

"There's a fine proctologist on the sixth floor. He'll be the man you want. Dr. Melvin, his name is."

Melvin didn't waste much time. "My God," he exclaimed irritably, after examining me. "What are you bothering me for? Your problem is a tooth problem, man. Now on the fifteenth floor, there's a dentist named Schoenfeld—"

And people wonder why I holler.

The public image of Alan King is, and was planned to be, that of a man who protests loudly. I've hollered so much that some people wonder how Jeanette puts up with it. Not long ago at a party somebody asked her about it, and I happened to overhear her reply.

"Alan?" she asked in amazement. "Why he's the nicest, sweetest guy in the whole world. Hollering is just his normal way of speaking. At heart he's a real softy—about his home, the boys, and me."

Now I've spent years developing my personality, and she takes about a minute to explain it all away. Could it be that this girl has my number?

Well, if a wife doesn't know, who does?

This book is dedicated with all my love and affection to my wife, Jeanette, who for fifteen years and 186 pages has taken all this with a smile.